How to Get Your First Job and Keep It

Deborah P. Bloch, Ph.D.

VGM Career Books

Chicago   New York   San Francisco   Lisbon   London   Madrid   Mexico City
Milan   New Delhi   San Juan   Seoul   Singapore   Sydney   Toronto

Library of Congress Cataloging-in-Publication Data

Bloch, Deborah Perlmutter.
    How to get your first job and keep it / Deborah P. Bloch. —2nd ed.
       p.   cm.
    Rev. ed. of: How to get a good job and keep it. New ed. c1993.
    Includes bibliographical references.
    ISBN 0-658-00620-7
    1. Job hunting.   2. Employment interviewing.   3. Success in business.
  I. Bloch, Deborah Perlmutter. How to get a good job and keep it.   II. Title.

HF5382.7 .B588   2002
650.14—dc21   2002022232

VGM Career Books

A Division of The McGraw·Hill Companies

This book was originally published as *How to Get a Good Job and Keep It.*

1 2 3 4 5 6 7 8 9 0 VLP/VLP 1 0 9 8 7 6 5 4 3 2

ISBN 0-658-00620-7

This book was set in New Century Schoolbook by JDA Typesetting Corporation
Printed and bound by Vicks Lithograph

Cover design by Amy Ng

McGraw-Hill books are available at special quantity discounts to use as premiums and sales promotions, or for use in corporate training programs. For more information, please write to the Director of Special Sales, Professional Publishing, McGraw-Hill, Two Penn Plaza, New York, NY 10121-2298. Or contact your local bookstore.

This book is printed on acid-free paper.

Contents

Introduction— Why You Want This Book

If you are reading this book—or even just looking at it— you are now ready for the world of full-time, paid work! You may be in high school thinking about the future in the next one, two, or three years. Perhaps you are about to graduate from college or a vocational program. Maybe you are a homemaker who wants to earn money for work. In any case, you are ready to move from the kind of work you have been doing to a different kind.

Both you and I know that you have been working all along, whether or not you've been paid for it. You've worked as a student and as a family member. You may have had part-time or temporary work. You may have done volunteer work in your community or religious organization. All of that work experience and what you learned from it will be part of the inner knowledge you draw upon as you learn how to get your first job and keep it.

Full-time work is often different from part-time work. The hiring process may be more complicated. Once hired, you may be expected to take on new or different responsibilities in the work place. This book will help you understand the ins and outs of getting hired, and then it will give you the needed clues about what employers really want on the job. You will have the information and confidence that you need to succeed.

In addition, you will find special sections to help you understand the use of computers in hiring and work. Computers are changing how we communicate both in writing and face-to-face. They are changing our sources of information, opening a wide array of sources we have never had before. And so the biggest challenge you face right now is how to use the right technology to maximize your ability to get the job that is right for you.

The most important thing to remember is that while technology has changed how we present ideas, human nature has not changed. Your prospective employer is still looking for the best person to do the job. He or she still has a mental image of the mix of education, skills, talents, and experiences that have shaped the ideal candidate. It is still your job to present what you know and what you can do to the best possible advantage. To help you take advantage of all technologies, from job searching on the Internet to using E-mail at work, a special section, "Techno-Tips," has been added to each chapter.

How to Get Your First Job and Keep It is divided into three parts. The first part is about getting the job. Look for Techno-Tips on information about occupations in general, about job listings, about scannable resumes, and about interviews through video-conferencing. The second part is about keeping that job, and what you can do on the first job to make it a successful experience. The emphasis here is on getting along well with others. In today's workplace, part of that is knowing how to use E-mail appropriately. Look for the Techno-Tips scenario on E-mail in the office. The third part is about moving on to your next job through promotion with the same employer or changing to a new employer. Look for Techno-Tips on using the company website.

Part I   Part I, "Getting the Job," is made up of four chapters. Each of these chapters deals with a different step in the process of finding a job.

Chapter 1, "How to Get Started," helps you understand the habits of successful people, and provides a checklist of what you need to know to launch a successful job search.

Chapter 2, "Places—Where Are the Jobs?" helps you identify sources of jobs and ways of making contact with agencies and people that have the jobs that interest you. In case you are not certain what interests you, this chapter also provides some information about how to get help in identifying your career choices. It even gives you a brief interest inventory to help you begin.

Chapter 3, " Papers—Applications, Resumes, and More," gives you concrete information on what to expect in filling out applications and provides you with worksheets that you can use ahead of time to prepare for any application. Some jobs require a resume and a cover letter to mail with it. Tests are required for some jobs. Helpful hints for successful test taking are given. All of the papers and forms you may need in your job hunt are listed and explained.

Chapter 4, "People—Seven Steps to a Winning Interview," helps you through this crucial process, the one that ensures you get a job. In this chapter you learn what to expect during an interview and how to prepare yourself for it.

Part II

Part II, "Keeping Your Job," is about succeeding on the job.

Chapter 5, "Hired!—Finding Out the Facts," gives you helpful hints on the kinds of information you want to find out from the company or organization that has hired you. The first part of the chapter deals with what you need to know before you accept a job offer. The second part helps with the first few days on the job. Having the right kinds of information will ensure that you and your boss or supervisor are operating on the same wavelength, that you have the same expectations about responsibilities and rewards, such as hours of work and paydays. You will learn how to fit in easily.

Chapter 6, "On-the-Job Success," is about the kinds of things you can do, and can avoid doing, on the job so that you are considered a valuable employee. Research has been done about what employers are looking for. This chapter lets you in on what employers have said about this. Through case studies, where you look at both the employee's and employer's points of view, you learn how to succeed. The chapter includes a checklist to help you organize your thinking.

Part III Part III, "Career Changes," is about the future.

Chapter 7, "Moving Up," helps you build on the success of your first job to move up. There are suggestions for getting raises and promotions within your company.

Chapter 8, "Moving On," provides tips on how to move to other organizations. The end of the chapter is about making your own opportunities and striking out on your own.

In all of the chapters, lots of worksheets and samples make this a practical book for your use. The book concludes with some additional sources of information.

GETTING THE JOB

Part I

How to Get Started 1

When you opened this book, you made an important decision. You decided to take charge of your life—right now. Figuring out the kind of work you want to do and can do, and then going for that first successful full-time job, is a major step.

Our jobs influence not only how much money we have to spend, but also how we spend our time and, very often, where we spend our lives. In carrying out a successful job search, you will draw on many experiences you have had in other aspects of your life. That's good! You will probably also learn a great deal about yourself, what you like, and what makes you tick. That's good as well. Finally, in the very act of finding a job, you will probably develop new skills and attitudes that you will be able to draw on in other situations.

Develop the Habits of Success

Successful job seekers and job keepers often have the habits of people who are successful in many areas of life. One of the most interesting books written about success is called, *The 7 Habits of Highly Effective People.* The author, Steven R. Covey, urged readers to determine what they want, figure out their goals and aim for them, put the most important things first, *and* do all of this while recognizing their interdependence with others.

The most important part of job seeking is determining your occupational goal. To do this you must think about your own interests, skills, needs, and abilities, and take a realistic look at the jobs available in the area where you want to live and work. Of course, sometimes this may mean you will have to compromise. You may decide you are willing to move to get the kind of job you want. On the other hand, you may not be willing to move, but you may decide to continue your education. Sometimes, we take one job while we seek the education we need to get the job we would rather have.

Once you have determined your goal, you need to put first things first. It would be nice to have a magic wand that would move us from choosing an occupation to working at it. But there are many steps in between. These steps include finding out about employers who have openings in the job title that interests you, filling out various papers, and being interviewed. That's only the short list. Each of the activities I mentioned will probably consist of several steps. But if you keep your eye on your goal, your persistence will pay off in a job.

In preparing for the job interview, you will see the wisdom of Covey's suggestion that you must "seek first to understand, then to be understood." As you will learn in the chapter on interviewing, listening is often the key to a successful interview. And you must have a successful interview to be hired. Understanding others—your coworkers, your boss, and anyone who reports to you—is the key to job success at any level. There will be more about interpersonal relations in the second part of this book.

Perhaps the most important of the "seven habits" is being *proactive*. Being proactive means going out and doing things for yourself. Of course, that includes getting the help you need from appropriate sources, and this book will help you identify those. But it can also mean getting help from more than one person or agency if that's what it takes.

A recent television program showed discouraged young men walking away from a factory. Each one had asked the first person they saw in the office, "Have you any job applications?" They were told "No," which was the truth. But, the employer said, "Why didn't they ask *when* applications *would* be available? Why didn't they ask for the manager's name so they could speak directly to her or him? Why didn't they show they cared about getting a job?" Now, it would be nice if that employer had been more concerned about others and had realized that inexperienced young people get nervous even asking for an application.

Yes, that employer could have been more helpful. But, once again, success comes down to helping yourself. If you are just trying to get your foot in the door, ask the same question many times in different ways. Ask for an application. Ask who has applications. Ask when applications will be available. Ask if applications are required. Remember all the no's still add up to only one no, but a single yes changes the picture entirely.

Learn the Skills of Job-Seeking Success

Many people are concerned right now about you and your future. That's because leaders in business, government, and education recognize how important it is for each and every one of us to find the job we want. This is important both for personal satisfaction and the country's economy.

For these reasons, the National Occupational Information Coordinating Committee, a federal agency, developed "The National Career Development Guidelines." These guidelines were developed for organizations that provide education and training at the elementary school, middle or junior high school, high school, and adult levels to help counselors, teachers, and administrators plan their programs. Organized programs are helpful, but self-help works too. What follows is a set of eleven indicators from the "Guidelines" for high school students and adults. They are called indicators because mastery of certain skills indicates that you are ready to conduct a successful job search.

Use the checklist to measure your strengths and weaknesses. It will help you understand what you need to concentrate on when using this book. Come back to the checklist as you work through the first part to see for yourself all that you have learned.

Ready to Find a Job
A Checklist of Indicators

Directions: In the first column, place a check next to those job-seeking skills you think you have "NOW." Place a question mark next to the ones you would like to find out more about. If you are uncertain, leave the space blank. As you read through this book, come back and place a plus sign in the second column, "LATER," when you think you have really mastered a particular skill.

Now	*Later*	*Essential Skills for Job Seeking*
____	____	1. Identify and appreciate personal interests, abilities, and skills
____	____	2. Describe how skills developed in academic and vocational programs relate to career goals.
____	____	3. Describe how educational achievements and life experiences relate to occupational opportunities.
____	____	4. Identify individuals in selected occupations as possible information resources, role models, or mentors.
____	____	5. Identify and use current career information resources, such as computerized career information systems and print materials.
____	____	6. Describe career planning and placement services available through organizations, for example, schools and colleges, business and industry, labor and community agencies.
____	____	7. Demonstrate skills to locate, interpret, and use information about job openings and opportunities.

____ ____   8. Demonstrate skills to establish a job-search network through colleagues, friends, and family.

____ ____   9. Demonstrate skills in preparing a resume and completing job applications.

____ ____   10. Demonstrate skills and behavior necessary for a successful job interview.

____ ____   11. Demonstrate skills to assess occupational opportunities, for example, working conditions, benefits, and opportunities for change.

Places—
Where Are
the Jobs?

You are ready to look for your first full-time, paid job. You have completed your education or training, or the part of it you plan to do now. Where do you go next? This chapter will help you identify the sources of jobs and how to use them. One of the most important things to remember in your job search is that you do not have to choose one method of searching or one agency to help you. You can use any or all of the ideas in this chapter so that you get the best possible job for you.

In the first section of the chapter you will find descriptions of various kinds of agencies and other sources of assistance that can help you in your job search. In the second section, you will learn how to use the newspaper and other advertisements and listings. Many people get jobs through people they know. The third section of this chapter helps you think about the people you know and how to get them to help you in your job search. The

9

fourth section of this chapter is for those who may be uncertain about the kind of job they want. There is a short interest inventory and some suggestions of other places to get help in narrowing the choice of jobs. Throughout the chapter look for Techno-Tips to help you in your search.

Helpful Agencies

A *school placement office* is probably available to you if you are now attending a high school, college, or trade school. If you have previously attended a college, you may be able to use the services of the placement office, often for a fee, even if you are no longer enrolled. The counselors in the school placement or counseling office can provide a number of services. They can help you figure out the kind of job you want and are qualified for; they can help you improve your resume-writing and interviewing skills; and they can help you identify actual job openings. Some schools arrange for recruiters to meet with potential employees.

It is important to remember that there are two worlds of jobs. One is the world of business, from small one-person operations to giant multinational corporations. The other is the world of government. Jobs in government—at the local, state, or federal level—are called civil service jobs. They include almost every kind of occupation there is. The school placement office will often have lists of both business and civil service job openings.

State employment services also run employment offices located in many areas within each state. You can find these by looking under state listings in your local telephone directory. Some *community or neighborhood organizations* offer job placement assistance. You can find out about these by looking in local papers or on bulletin boards in libraries and other public places. These employment services will provide information about business job openings and civil service job listings.

Private employment agencies work for the employer who pays the fees. From your point of view, the agency is helping you find a job. From the employer's point of view, the agency is helping fill a vacant position. In most cases this works out just fine. When you look at newspaper advertisements for jobs, you will see that many of them are placed by private employment agencies to which you can apply. You will also find listings of private employment agencies in your local classified telephone directory.

Private Career Counseling Services

These services help you assess your goals and develop resume-writing and interviewing skills, the kinds of skills presented in this book and others like it. However, many of these career counseling services do not provide job placement. The National Career Development Association, a professional organization of counselors, has prepared consumer guidelines for selecting a career counselor.

Guidelines for Selecting a Career Counselor*

Sometimes it seems that virtually everyone is a vocational coach, ready and eager to give advice, suggestions, and directions. Unfortunately, all are not equally able to provide the kind of help people need in making decisions about what to do with their lives. Promises and luxurious trappings are poor substitutes for competency. Thus, the selection of a professional career counselor is a very important task. The following guidelines are offered to assist you in making the selection.

Credentials of the professional career counselor

A Nationally Certified Career Counselor is a counselor who has achieved the highest certification in the profession. Further, it means that the career counselor has

- earned a graduate degree in counseling or in a related professional field from a regionally accredited higher education institution.

- completed supervised counseling experience which included career counseling.

- acquired a minimum of three years of full-time career development work experience.

- obtained written endorsements of competence in career counseling from a work supervisor and a professional colleague.

- successfully completed a knowledge-based certification examination.

---

*These guidelines were produced by the National Career Development Association and are reprinted with their permission.

Other professional counselors may be trained in one- or two-year counselor preparation programs with specialties in career counseling, and may be licensed or certified by national or state professional associations.

What do career counselors do?

The services of career counselors differ, depending on competence. A professional or Nationally Certified Career Counselor helps people make decisions and plans related to life/career directions. The strategies and techniques are tailored to the specific needs of the person seeking help. It is likely that the career counselor will do one or more of the following:

- conduct individual and group personal counseling sessions to help clarify life/career goals.

- administer and interpret tests and inventories to assess abilities, interests, etc., and to identify career options.

- encourage exploratory activities through assignments and planning experiences.

- utilize career planning systems and occupational information systems to help individuals better understand the world of work.

- provide opportunities for improving decision-making skills.

- assist in developing individualized career plans.

- teach job-hunting strategies and skills, and assist in the development of resumes.

- help resolve potential personal conflicts on the job through practice in human relations skills.

- assist in understanding the integration of work and other life roles.

- provide support for persons experiencing job stress, job loss or career transition.

Ask for a detailed explanation of services provided (such as career counseling, testing, employment search strategy planning and resume writing). Make sure you understand the service, and your degree of involvement and financial commitment.

Fees

Select a counselor who is professionally trained and will let you choose the services you desire. Make certain you can terminate the services at any time, paying only for services rendered.

Promises

Be skeptical of services that make promises of more money, better jobs, resumes that get speedy results or an immediate solution to career problems.

Ethical practices

A professional or Nationally Certified Career Counselor is expected to follow the ethical guidelines of such organizations as The National Career Development Association, The American Association for Counseling and Development, and The American Psychological Association, Professional codes of ethics advise against grandiose guarantees and promises, exorbitant fees, and breaches of confidentiality, among other things. You may wish to ask for a detailed explanation of services offered, your expected financial and time commitments, and a copy of the ethical guidelines used by the career counselor you are considering.

Techno-Tips

> ### National Career Development Association Online
>
> Additional information about the qualifications and services of career counselors can be found on the website of the National Career Development Association at ncda.org. The website also provides information on how to find a career counselor in your area.

Other Sources of Assistance

Human resource management departments of large companies sometimes accept job applications on an ongoing basis. First, you need to figure out the kinds of companies that need the kind of work you do. It is pretty obvious that if you are looking for a job as a sales clerk, you can go to a department store, but the relationship between many jobs and industries is not always clear. In school placement offices and libraries, you can find career information in computer-based systems and in books such as the *Occupational Outlook Handbook.* In the description of the job that interests you, you will find descriptions of the industries in which that job is found. Knowledge of the industries can help you determine which companies in your area may need your work. If you need help understanding these connections, counselors and librarians can often provide it.

You can then identify the companies in your area on your own by asking a counselor or by looking in the classified yellow pages telephone directory. Be sure to read the section in Chapter 3 on completing job applications. Then go to the company's human resources department and ask to complete an application.

Techno-Tips

The *Occupational Outlook Handbook* Online

You can use the *Occupational Outlook Handbook (OOH)* online by going to bls.gov/oco/home. This valuable resource has been published by the Bureau of Labor Statistics of the U.S. Department of Labor since 1949. The *OOH* provides descriptions of approximately two hundred fifty occupations including working conditions, qualifications, and outlook for the future. The occupations included in the *OOH* include almost all of the occupations available in the United States as well as in most other industrialized countries. While the print and online versions contain the same information, the online version allows you to search the information by key words, by index, and by job clusters.

For each occupation, you will find sections that help you answer the following questions:

- What does a person do on the job? Look at Nature of the Work.

- Where is the work done? During what hours? What are the physical demands? Look at Working Conditions.

- How many people work at this job in the United States? In what industries do people work? Look at Employment.

- What do I need to know to get this job and get ahead in it? Look at Training, Other Qualifications, and Advancement.

- Will there be many or few openings for this job in the next eight to ten years? Look at Job Outlook?

- How much money am I likely to earn? Look at Earnings.

- What other occupations call for similar tasks and skills? Look at Related Occupations.

- Where can I get more information about this occupation? Look at Sources of Additional Information.

Military recruitment offices fall into a unique category of employment agency because taking a job in the military is different in many ways from taking a job in civilian employment. If you are considering the military as a first job, remember that there are different services that compete with each other, and the job of the recruiter is to get you to join the service he or she represents. One book that covers all the bases is *America's Top Military Careers*, compiled by the United States Department of Defense. If you are thinking about a career or a job in the military, be sure to read this book or search online for other reliable information.

Although all of these agencies can be helpful to you in your job search, there are differences among them that you should be aware of. The placement office in your school works for you. You are the customer whether the service is free or not. The school placement office counselors are interested in placing you in the best job they can.

Employment agencies, on the other hand, work for the companies with job vacancies. That is why you pay no placement fee. The fee is paid by the company. Their interest, therefore, is not in helping you but in finding the best possible person for the job. That does not mean that they will not be helpful to you. It does mean that you need to know their point of view.

State employment services are more neutral. Their goal is to make as many placements as possible so that fewer people are unemployed and the economy of the state is healthy. The range of services provided by the state employment service varies from state to state.

The private career counseling services work for you, the client, and you usually pay a fee. Some career counseling services will help you find a job, but most provide other services, so be sure to read Guidelines for Selecting a Career Counselor that appears earlier in this chapter if you want to get help from a career counselor.

Find the employment services most suited to your needs. Use them to identify job leads and to get any help offered in presenting yourself on a job. You need not stick to one choice. You can go to your school placement office, the state employment service, and register with several employment agencies. Before you sign any agreements with an employment service, be sure you know the following:

1. Is there a fee?

2. How much is the fee and who is responsible for it?

3. If you are paying, what is the agency promising to do?

Use the Employment Service Checklist that follows to identify and keep track of the services you are planning to use.

Employment Service Checklist

Check the types of services that are available and useful to you. Then fill in the actual names of the agencies and the information about them as you identify them.

Type	Name and Address	Fees	Services
___ School Placement Office	_____	___	_____
	_____	___	_____
	_____	___	_____
___ State Employment Service	_____	___	_____
	_____	___	_____
	_____	___	_____
___ Community Agency 1	_____	___	_____
	_____	___	_____
	_____	___	_____
___ Community Agency 2	_____	___	_____
	_____	___	_____
	_____	___	_____
___ Employment Agency 1	_____	___	_____
	_____	___	_____
	_____	___	_____
___ Employment Agency 2	_____	___	_____
	_____	___	_____
	_____	___	_____
___ Human Resource Management Department 1	_____	___	_____
	_____	___	_____
	_____	___	_____

____ Human Resource Management
Department 2

_____   ___   _____

_____   ___   _____

_____   ___   _____

____ Career Counselor

_____   ___   _____

_____   ___   _____

_____   ___   _____

____ Military Recruitment Office

_____   ___   _____

_____   ___   _____

_____   ___   _____

Advertisements and Listings

Answering an advertisement may lead to your first job. You can find job advertisements in your local newspaper in the classified section and often in specialized sections for business, education, and health. Several major newspapers, like the *New York Times* and the *Wall Street Journal,* carry ads for national companies. If you are interested in working for a large organization, you will want to check the ads in one or both of these while you are job hunting. You will also find ads in professional newspapers and magazines. Of course, these are jobs related to the interests of the readers.

Some advertisements call for a written answer. To answer such an ad, you will need to prepare your resume and write a cover letter. Chapter 3 gives you help in resume preparation. Other advertisements ask that you call. You will find help in making telephone arrangements in Chapter 4.

Newspaper advertisements are listed alphabetically by job title. However, some of these titles are not very specific. For example, there is often a large section listed as *college grad.* The first thing to do is to go through the newspaper for several days and write down *all* of the job titles that could be right for you. It is much better to apply for some jobs that are not appropriate than to miss the one that is right. Be sure to look most closely at the Sunday papers. Many more ads are usually found there.

Some job ads are placed directly by the employer, others by employment agencies. Employment agency ads usually list the name of the agency and contain some phrase like "fee paid" or "f/pd," which means that the employer pays the agency fee. Job advertisements are often written in a peculiar shorthand to save space and the money it costs. Here are two recent advertisements and their translations. After that, you will find a list of commonly used abbreviations and their meanings.

SAMPLE JOB ADVERTISEMENT 1
GAL/GUY FRIDAY
Acts rec, type 60wpm, gd telephone voice, word pring & database mgmt knldg helpful. Midtown loc. Call Gary btwn 10-4, 555-2378.

TRANSLATION OF JOB ADVERTISEMENT 1

A person who is able and willing to do a variety of office tasks is needed. The person will work on some bookkeeping with accounts receivable, must be able to type 60 words per minute, and must be able to speak clearly on the telephone. It would be helpful if he or she also knows how to use a computer for word processing and database management. The job is located in the midtown area. If you are interested, call the number given between 10 in the morning and 4 in the afternoon and ask for Gary. [This ad was placed by the company itself. No starting salary is mentioned.]

SAMPLE JOB ADVERTISEMENT 2
College Grad   f/pd   24–28K
Prestig cos have several entry level openings for indivs w/interest in pr/advtg. Candidate should be articulate and possess interpersonal skills. Typg reqd. WP a +, gd benefits, tuition. Call Mr. Horton, 555-8787.

TRANSLATION OF JOB ADVERTISEMENT 2

This ad was placed by an employment agency and groups several jobs that the agency is trying to fill. Although the jobs are for college graduates with an interest in public relations and advertising, the employee will be working, at least part of the time, as a typist. In fact, knowledge of word processing is a plus, or a help in getting the job. The jobs are with well-known companies and have good benefits, usually health insurance and paid vacation, in addition to the salary. Tuition will be paid for additional education. This usually means for education related to the job functions.

List of advertisement abbreviations

Following is a list of commonly used abbreviations and their meanings. However, there really is no complete list. The best trick is to try reading the ad aloud, filling in letters to make all the abbreviated words complete.

Abbreviation	Translation
a +	a plus (if you have this, you are a better candidate)
acctg	accounting
advc	advancement
agcy	agency

appt	appointment
asst	assistant
begnr	beginner
bkpg	bookkeeping
bnfts	benefits
clk	clerk
co	company (mjr co means major company)
col grad	college graduate
dept	department
dict	dictation
EOE	Equal Opportunity Employer
eves	evenings
exp nec	experience necessary
exp pfd	experience preferred
f/pd	fee paid
f/t	full-time
gd	good
immed	immediate or immediately
inq	inquire
K	thousands (usually annual salary in dollars)
loc	location or located
mfg	manufacturing
mgmt	management
ovtm	overtime (sometimes written o/t)
opty	opportunity
ofc	office
pd vac	paid vacation
p/t	part-time
refs	references
secty	secretary
sr	senior (usually means experienced)
w/	with (w/wo means with or without)
wkend	weekend
wpm	words per minute
yr	year

Techno-Tips

Job Openings

The Internet or World Wide Web is an excellent source of information about jobs in general and about particular corporations and other organizations. You can use this information to begin the broad search for occupations of interest and use it to conclude your search by

---

actually finding a job posting, submitting your resume electronically, and even interviewing online from your home or from a special site that has been set up to communicate with one or many employers.

You can use the power of the Internet to help you identify your ideal working conditions. The Internet provides you with many more sources of information about occupations and jobs than you could get through print alone. Sometimes in using the Internet, however, it seems that sites appear and disappear. To some extent this is true, just as it is true that some businesses have long lives and some go under quickly. Because of this changeable nature of the Internet, I hesitate to provide specific addresses—or URLs—in this book. However, there are several sites that have had longevity and may prove of continuing use.

The first site, CAREERMOSAIC, which can be found at careermosaic.com, is a privately run Internet career resource center with many links within it. It has job listings as well as tips on using the Internet for job searching and resume writing. Another site, hotjobs.com, lists jobs in technology in more than one hundred companies. The job ads from forty-five (at this writing) newspapers are listed on careerpath.com. And monster.com provides another database of jobs.

Governments at all levels—city, state, and federal—are major employers in the United States. You can now find listings of civil service jobs on special websites for each state. These sites often have the most up-to-date listings of upcoming jobs. Since these are government jobs, the application procedures will be very specific. You can usually find all you need to know right on the site. Sometimes, however, you will also be asked to call or write for the actual application or other materials.

Here's how to find the civil service site for your state. Go to a search engine such as google.com. You will see a box to enter the information you want and a "Search" button. In the box enter the name of the state that interests you and the words *civil service,* all in quotation marks. For example, enter "Florida Civil Service" and click on the search button. You will then get a list of matches. It is likely that the first item on the list may be the one you want, but you may need to read down the list to find the right site. This sometimes takes patience. If you go to a listing that is not useful, use the "Back" button at the top of the screen to go back to the list.

You can also go from general sites like CAREER-MOSAIC to the sites of particular organizations. You will get some of the Web addresses from links to sites like CAREERMOSAIC. In addition, most organizations now list their URLs in all promotional materials they circulate. You can also use a Web browser, such as Google, to search the Internet for words or phrases that name a corporation. And finally, you can take a stab at how a major organization may list itself. For example, if you are looking for information by and about Wobbly Widgets, you can try entering "wobbly.com" or "wobbly.widgets.com" or "wobblywidgets.com." By experimenting, you can often find a combination that works.

Getting Help from People You Know

Networking is a popular term that gives a technical sound to a technique that people have been using for a very long time. Basically, it means that you tell all the people you know that you are looking for a job and ask them to help you. Do not think that you do not know anybody who can help you. Think of the word *network*. Picture a network. It is not a single string from you to one person and another from you to another person. It is like a web with strings from you to the people you know and from them to the people they know. People generally like to help others. One reason is because it makes them feel good. The other is because it increases their own net work of people they know.

The first thing to do is to make a list of everyone you know. Consider people from all aspects of your life: family; friends; parents or children of friends; teachers; fellow members of religious, professional, and community organizations; and sports teammates or opponents.

The next step is to think of what you want from each of these people. How can each one help you? Some may actually be employed by or run organizations in which you would like to work. Others may know people in the kinds of organizations you would like to work for. Still others may be just a shot in the dark. That is, you can't think of how they can help you, but it's worth seeing if they can. Your approach to each person may have to be a little different. You will be able to speak directly to some people when you see them in the course of everyday affairs. You may need to telephone or write others.

Try to be as direct and specific as you can in your approach. Say something like "I am graduating from community college with a degree in office management. I will be ready to start work the first of February. If you can think of anywhere I might apply or anyone I should speak to, I would appreciate it."

If that's not like your situation at all, say something like "I am graduating from high school, and I will be looking for a job where I can do a lot of outdoor work. I really don't mind moving around and lifting heavy things. You know, I've done a lot of that around the house for the last few years. If you can think of any openings I might apply for or anyone I should speak to, please let me know."

Maybe that still doesn't sound right for you. You may want to try something like "I'm looking for a job in sales where I can use some of those persuasive skills I have learned in all those volunteer fundraisers for the community center. Do you know anyone looking for a mature, skilled salesperson? I would really appreciate any leads you could give me."

One of the most important techniques for a job search is keeping records of what you have done and where it has led. This is particularly important in networking since one contact may lead to another. Here is an example of the kind of record you could keep for networking:

Networking Records

SAMPLE: Name <u>Lois Rich</u>
Address <u>Ferry Road, Bristol, RI</u>
Telephone <u>(401) 555-2664 (work)</u>
Source of Contact <u>Friend of Uncle Paul</u>
Method of Contact <u>I telephoned her at work.</u>
Date(s) of Contact <u>2/17</u>
Results/Follow-up <u>She asked me to send her a resume.</u>
<u>Sent 2/19. Call her 2/28.</u>

CONTACT 1:   Name _____
Address _____
Telephone _____
Source of Contact _____
Method of Contact _____
Date(s) of Contact _____
Results/Follow-up _____
_____
_____

CONTACT 2:   Name _____
Address _____
Telephone _____
Source of Contact _____
Method of Contact _____
Date(s) of Contact _____
Results/Follow-up _____
_____
_____

CONTACT 3:   Name _____
Address _____
Telephone _____
Source of Contact _____
Method of Contact _____
Date(s) of Contact _____
Results/Follow-up _____
_____
_____

CONTACT 4: Name _____
Address _____
Telephone _____
Source of Contact _____
Method of Contact _____
Date(s) of Contact _____
Results/Follow-up _____
_____
_____

CONTACT 5: Name _____
Address _____
Telephone _____
Source of Contact _____
Method of Contact _____
Date(s) of Contact _____
Results/Follow-up _____
_____
_____

CONTACT 6: Name _____
Address _____
Telephone _____
Source of Contact _____
Method of Contact _____
Date(s) of Contact _____
Results/Follow-up _____
_____
_____

CONTACT 7: Name _____
Address _____
Telephone _____
Source of Contact _____
Method of Contact _____
Date(s) of Contact _____
Results/Follow-up _____
_____
_____

Choosing an Occupation

Some people looking for their first job know what they want to do. Others are not as certain. If you have graduated from high school and you have not taken particular courses in a business or vocational area, or if you are graduating from college with a major in a liberal arts or science discipline, you may need some help in making a career choice. Even if you have studied a subject that leads to a particular occupation, that may not be the occupation that now interests you.

Few people choose an occupation and stick to it for life. It has been estimated that most people make three to four career changes in their lives; that's not just job changes, but changes in direction. If you are in the position of making a choice at this time, there are a number of sources of help for you.

At the beginning of this chapter, several types of agencies that provide job placement assistance were identified. A number of these also provide help with choosing a career. If you are still in high school or college, there is almost certainly a counseling office to help you. That is a good place to begin. Some state employment services also offer testing. Sometimes this is available only to certain groups, such as those between 16 and 21 years of age, or those who are starting to work after being homemakers. Your local telephone directory will lead you to your state employment service.

In addition, some community agencies and universities offer career counseling. You can find out about these through local libraries, from your clergyman, or by contacting a state university directly. The private career counseling services mentioned earlier may prove helpful. Be sure to ascertain the qualifications of the counselors in any private service, using the guidelines included earlier in this chapter.

Some people prefer to work through the process of career decision making on their own. If you would like to do that, there are some things you can do. Your local library or community college may provide access to a computer-based career information delivery system. These systems help you develop a list of careers that meet your interests, needs, and abilities. The systems then provide information on the careers, their entry-level requirements, the opportunities for advancement, and the industries in which they are most often found. Some systems will even provide information on specific employers in your state or region of the state.

At the end of this section, you will find a set of questions and answers—The Skills Assessment Questionnaire, adapted from Quest, the exploratory part of the Career Information System. The Career Information System is in use in sixteen states, so you may be able to find it at your school or library. You can take The Skills Assessment Questionnaire and see what occupations it suggests for you. You can then use the Career Information System, or another computer-based career information delivery system, to get information on the occupations or to continue your self-assessment.

If you do not have access to a Career Information System, your counselor or librarian can help you get more information about any occupations that interest you. There are a number of books that can help you in this process. The *Occupational Outlook Handbook* provides excellent brief descriptions of jobs. If you want to read more about a particular occupation or industry, look for books like those in the *Opportunities in . . .* series published by VGM Career Books. *What Color Is Your Parachute* by Richard Nelson Bolles (Ten Speed Press) gives techniques for career choosing that have been used successfully by many people. Another book you might find helpful is *SoulWork: Finding the Work You Love, Loving the Work You Have.* This book helps you think about your skills and abilities as well as your needs and interests, or in other words, your calling. It also helps you figure out how to find work that harmonizes with your calling.

Remember, The Skills Assessment Questionnaire is just a way to get started thinking about your first job choice if you haven't already done so. It contains only about one hundred occupations, while the Career Information System contains more than three hundred. For example, all of the careers requiring graduate study for a first job, such as lawyers and doctors, have been left out of the Skills Assessment Questionnaire. This version is not really designed for long-range planning. It is to help you identify some first job choices that require, at most, a four-year college degree.

The Skills Assessment Questionnaire

The Skills Assessment Questionnaire* that follows consists of sixteen items. Think about each skill, and decide whether this is a skill you possess and if you would like to use it on a job. For example, the first skill listed deals with the ability to do continuous work. Decide if you are able to do continuous work; ask yourself if you want to. If the answer to both questions is *yes* mark Item 1 "yes." If you cannot do continuous work, or prefer not to, mark Item 1 "no."

After you answer the sixteen questions, turn to the Job Matching Section, which immediately follows. Fill in the circles at the top of the first page to match your "yes" answers to the sixteen questions. This is your skills profile. The skills profile for each job has already been filled in. Go down the pages, job by job, and note the number of matches between your skills profile and each job's. You will then be able to see which jobs match your strengths and interests.

1. *Continuous:*
   On some jobs you do the same things many times a day and you work at a steady pace. Is this type of work for you? ____ YES   ____ NO

2. *Precise:*
   On some jobs there is little room for error so you must be very exact in your work. Is this type of work for you? ____ YES   ____ NO

3. *Using Facts:*
   On some jobs you use factual information to decide what to do. Is this type of work for you?
   ____ YES   ____ NO

4. *Working with Others:*
   On some jobs you must deal with many different people to get your work done. Is this type of work for you? ____ YES   ____ NO

5. *Persuading:*
   On some jobs you talk with people to try to influence other people's actions or ideas. Is this type of work for you? ____ YES   ____ NO

6. *Decision Making:*
   On some jobs you are responsible for making major decisions about projects, plans, and other people's duties. Is this type of work for you? ____ YES   ____ NO

7. *Change:*
   On some jobs you must move often from one task to another and use several different skills. Is this type of work for you? ____ YES   ____ NO

---

*The Skills Assessment Questionnaire is an adaptation of Quest, copyrighted by the National Career Information System, University of Oregon, 1987, and is used with their permission.

8. *Creative:*
  On some jobs you must express feelings and ideas in artistic ways. Is this type of work for you?
____ YES   ____ NO

9. *Eye-Hand Coordination:*
  On some jobs you need to be very good at handling objects quickly as you see them. Is this type of work for you? ____ YES   ____ NO

10. *Working with Fingers:*
  On some jobs you need to be able to do very precise work with your fingers. You need to work with small things very quickly and carefully. Is this type of work for you?
____ YES   ____ NO

11. *Checking Accuracy:*
  On some jobs you need to be very accurate at reading or copying written materials. You have to be very good at things like proofreading numbers and words. Is this type of work for you?
____ YES   ____ NO

12. *Use of Words:*
  On some jobs you need to be able to read and understand instructions easily. You have to express yourself very clearly in writing, or when talking with people. Is this type of job for you?
____ YES   ____ NO

13. *Use of Numbers:*
  On some jobs you need to be able to work very quickly and accurately with numbers or measurements. Is this type of work for you? ____ YES   ____ NO

14. *Catching On to Things:*
  On some jobs you need the ability to understand procedures and the reasonings behind them. You have to be very good at figuring out complicated things quickly and easily. Is this type of work for you? ____ YES   ____ NO

15. *Seeing Detail:*
  On some jobs you need to be able to tell slight differences in shapes of objects and lengths of lines. You have to be able to see detail in objects, pictures, or drawings. Is this type of work for you? ____ YES   ____ NO

16. *Physical Activity:*
  Jobs require different amounts of physical activity. On some jobs you need to be very active, often handling twenty-five-pound objects and sometimes more. Is this type of work for you?
____ YES   ____ NO

Job Matching Section

Your Skills Profile:

• JOB TITLES •	✓	1 CONTINUOUS	2 PRECISE	3 USING FACTS	4 WORKING WITH OTHERS	5 PERSUADING WITH OTHERS	6 DECISION MAKING	7 CHANGE	8 CREATIVE	9 EYE-HAND COORDINATION	10 WORKING WITH FINGERS	11 CHECKING ACCURACY	12 USE OF WORDS	13 USE OF NUMBERS	14 CATCHING ON TO THINGS	15 SEEING DETAIL	16 PHYSICAL ACTIVITY
Accountants & Auditors			•	•			•					•	•	•	•		
Animal Caretakers						•		•	•		•		•		•		•
Air Traffic Controllers			•				•	•			•	•	•	•	•		
Bakers			•						•	•				•	•	•	
Bank Tellers		•	•		•				•	•	•	•	•	•	•		
Bartenders				•						•			•				
Body & Fender Repairers			•	•			•		•			•	•	•		•	•
Bookkeepers			•						•	•	•	•	•	•	•		
Building Maintenance Workers			•				•		•	•		•	•	•		•	•
Bus & Taxi Drivers				•	•				•			•		•			•
Buyers					•	•	•	•			•	•	•	•	•		
Carpenters			•	•				•		•	•		•		•	•	•
Cashiers		•	•		•				•	•	•	•	•	•			
Cement Masons			•	•				•					•		•	•	•
Chefs & Cooks			•				•		•		•	•	•	•	•	•	•
Child Care Workers					•		•				•		•		•		•
Claims Adjusters & Examiners			•	•						•	•	•	•				
Coal & Mineral Mining Occupations		•	•						•			•					
Commercial Artists							•	•	•	•	•	•	•	•	•	•	
Commercial Fishers		•															•
Computer Operators			•					•		•	•	•	•	•	•		
Computer Programmers			•	•							•	•	•	•	•		
Construction Laborers		•	•														•
Data Entry Operators		•	•						•	•	•	•		•	•		
Dental Hygienists			•		•				•	•		•	•	•	•		
Designers, Clothes			•	•					•	•	•	•	•	•	•		
Designers, Floral					•			•	•	•	•	•	•	•	•		
Designers, Interior					•	•	•		•	•	•	•	•	•	•		
Drafters			•	•					•	•	•	•	•	•	•		

	NUMBER OF MATCHES	CONTINUOUS	PRECISE	USING FACTS	WORKING WITH OTHERS	PERSUADING	DECISION MAKING	CHANGE	CREATIVE	EYE-HAND COORDINATION	WORKING WITH FINGERS	CHECKING ACCURACY	USE OF WORDS	USE OF NUMBERS	CATCHING ON TO THINGS	SEEING DETAIL	PHYSICAL ACTIVITY
Electricians			•	•			•			•	•		•	•	•	•	•
Electronics Assemblers	•	•	•							•	•					•	
Engineers			•	•			•	•		•	•	•	•	•	•	•	
Farmers & Ranchhands			•				•	•		•			•	•	•	•	
Firefighters							•		•	•			•				•
Foresters			•	•			•	•		•	•	•	•				
Freight Handlers	•								•								•
General Office Clerks		•								•	•	•	•	•	•		
Groundskeepers & Gardeners		•															•
Hair Stylists				•			•		•	•			•		•	•	
Handcrafters		•						•	•	•				•	•	•	•
Health & Safety Inspectors		•	•	•								•	•	•	•		
Heavy Equipment Operators		•							•	•					•	•	•
Hotel Desk Clerks			•				•			•	•	•	•	•	•		
Interpreters & Translators			•	•						•	•		•				
Jewelers			•	•			•			•	•		•	•	•	•	
Laundry & Dry Cleaning Workers		•															•
Law Enforcement Officers				•			•		•	•	•		•		•	•	•
Legal Assistants		•	•	•			•					•	•	•	•		
Library Assistants				•			•		•	•	•		•		•	•	•
Machinists		•	•				•		•	•			•	•	•	•	•
Meat Cutters		•	•						•	•				•	•	•	•
Mechanics, Automobile		•	•				•		•	•	•		•	•	•	•	•
Mechanics, Heavy Equipment		•	•				•		•	•		•	•	•	•	•	•
Medical Laboratory Workers		•	•				•		•	•		•	•	•	•		
Messengers	•			•													
Metal Refining Occupations	•	•															•
Nurses Aides & Orderlies				•			•										•
Nurses (LPN)		•		•			•		•	•			•		•	•	•
Nurses (RN)		•	•	•			•		•	•	•	•	•	•	•	•	
Office Machine Repairers		•	•				•		•	•		•	•	•	•	•	•
Packers & Wrappers	•								•	•							•
Painters & Paperhangers		•							•	•		•	•	•	•	•	•
Performing Artists									•	•	•		•	•	•	•	

	NUMBER OF MATCHES	CONTINUOUS	PRECISE	USING FACTS	WORKING WITH OTHERS	PERSUADING	DECISION MAKING	CHANGE	CREATIVE	EYE-HAND COORDINATION	WORKING WITH FINGERS	CHECKING ACCURACY	USE OF WORDS	USE OF NUMBERS	CATCHING ON TO THINGS	SEEING DETAIL	PHYSICAL ACTIVITY
Personnel Officers			•	•			•					•	•	•	•		
Petroleum Processing Occupations			•	•								•	•	•			
Photographers			•		•				•	•		•	•	•	•		
Plumbers & Pipefitters			•	•				•		•		•	•	•	•	•	•
Printing Production Occupations			•	•				•		•	•	•	•	•	•		
Production Assemblers	•	•								•	•					•	
Public Relations Workers					•	•	•	•	•			•	•	•	•	•	
Pulp & Paper Workers			•	•						•		•		•	•		
Railroad Conductors			•	•		•	•			•	•				•		
Recreation Attendants			•							•	•	•	•				
Salespeople				•	•				•			•	•	•	•		
Secretaries		•		•				•		•	•	•	•	•	•	•	
Security Guards	•			•											•		
Service Station Attendants				•				•				•	•	•	•	•	•
Shipping & Receiving Clerks			•	•				•			•	•	•	•	•	•	
Shoe Repairers			•	•					•	•		•			•	•	
Social Service Aides				•				•			•	•	•	•			
Social Workers				•	•	•						•	•	•			
Surveyor Helpers	•	•															•
Teacher Aides				•				•			•	•	•	•			
Teachers				•	•	•	•				•	•	•	•	•		
Technicians, Broadcast		•	•						•	•		•	•	•	•		
Technicians, Computer Maintenance		•	•	•		•	•		•	•		•	•	•	•		
Technicians, Dental Laboratory		•	•					•		•	•	•	•	•	•		
Technicians, Emergency Medical			•	•					•	•	•	•	•	•	•	•	•
Technicians, Engineering		•	•						•	•	•	•	•	•	•		
Technicians, Fish & Wildlife			•					•	•	•					•		•
Technicians, Health		•	•	•					•	•	•	•	•	•	•		
Technicians, Nuclear Power		•	•					•		•	•	•	•	•	•		•
Technicians, Solar		•	•					•		•	•		•	•	•	•	•
Telephone & Teletype Operators	•			•					•	•	•	•			•		
Telephone Installers & Repairers		•	•	•				•		•	•		•	•	•	•	
Textile Machine Operators	•	•															•
Therapists, Physical			•	•	•	•	•			•	•	•	•	•	•	•	

	Number of Matches	Continuous	Precise	Using Facts	Working with Others	Persuading	Decision Making	Change	Creative	Eye-Hand Coordination	Working with Fingers	Checking with Accuracy	Use of Words	Use of Numbers	Catching On to Things	Seeing Detail	Physical Activity
Travel Agents					•	•						•	•	•	•		
Truck Drivers		•								•	•				•	•	•
Upholsterers			•	•						•	•	•	•	•	•	•	•
Waiters & Waitresses					•						•		•				
Welders			•	•						•	•	•		•	•	•	•
Woodworking Machine Operators		•	•							•					•	•	•
Word Processors			•							•	•	•	•	•	•	•	
Writers & Editors				•	•			•	•			•	•	•	•	•	

Summary Worksheet

In this chapter, you have examined the sources of jobs and information about jobs. Use this summary worksheet to be sure you have left no stone unturned in your job search.

_____ I have identified agencies that can help me in my job search. They are: _____

_____

_____

_____ I have thought about companies I can apply to directly. They are: _____

_____

_____

_____ I know the headings in newspapers under which I can look for jobs that interest me. They include:

_____

_____

_____ I know how to read newspaper advertisements.

_____ I have identified some people I know who can help me. They are: _____

_____

_____ I know how to use the Internet for information about occupations in general.

_____ I know how to use the Internet to find out about specific jobs.

_____ I know what job I am seeking or how to go about figuring that out.

Papers— Applications, Resumes, and More

3

There are two keys to a successful job hunt—one is dealing with paper, the other involves people. This chapter is about paper. Of course, today not all paper records are actually handled on paper that you can see and touch. A lot of it is electronic in nature, so this chapter will contain Techno-Tips on using technology to create and send your "paper" resumes.

In many cases, employers see the papers you have prepared about yourself long before they meet you. You will fill out an application or send in a resume. Based on that application or resume you will be called to the next step, the interview, or you will be eliminated. Often the same is true after you leave the interview. Your application or resume is left behind as the only concrete reminder of your skills and personality. This chapter will help you present yourself in the best possible light so that your strengths stand out on paper and the very appearance of the papers themselves show how well organized you are.

The first section of this chapter provides directions on how to complete job applications and the information you should have on hand whenever you expect to complete one. The second section gives you suggestions for preparing your resume and cover letter and provides examples that you can use as models. Some jobs, particularly civil service jobs, require tests. The third section of this chapter gives you some hints on taking tests. In the fourth section of the chapter, helpful hints on items to take with you on your job hunt are given.

How to Complete Job Applications

Although many companies have job applications that are made particularly for them, most applications ask for the same information. In general, this includes the following:

- Location information—your name, address, and telephone number; and the name, address, and telephone number of someone to contact in an emergency

- Your Social Security number

- Job desired—the name of the position for which you are applying, are you looking for full-time or part-time work, the date you are available for work, the salary you expect, the source of your application or how you heard of the company, relatives who work for the company

- Education information—the degrees you have, where you went to school, when you graduated, what you majored in

- Work history—jobs you have held, when you held them, where you worked

- Special skills and talents—typing ability, knowledge of foreign languages, hobbies, volunteer work, sports, honors and awards in school

- References—the names and addresses of three people who can discuss your strengths and abilities

- Citizenship and military service

- Criminal records

As soon as you decide to apply for a job you need to be prepared to complete an application. You may be going to a company office because one of the employment services suggested in Chapter 2 has sent you to apply for a job; you may be going because you identified the company as one that has the kind of work you want to do; or you may be going because you are answering a newspaper ad. Here are six tips for completing a job application.

Six tips for completing a job application

1. Have all your information prepared ahead of time and carry it with you so that you know the answers to all the questions that apply to you. **Be accurate.**

2. Always apply for a specific job title. In the space "Position Desired," never write "anything." There is no job called "anything," so no one will know what to do with your application. **Be definite.**

3. Answer all questions honestly. **Be honest.**

4. Don't leave any blanks. If a question does not apply to you, write "No" or "None" or "Not Applicable." **Be complete.**

5. Sometimes you are asked to complete your work history or education history in chronological order; this means you start with the first and move to the most recent. Sometimes you are asked for reverse chronological order; this means you start with the most recent and present things going backward in time. **Read directions.**

6. Complete the application in ink. Carry a pen with an ink eraser or even some correction fluid. **Neatness counts.**

In the following pages, you will find three worksheets to help you complete job applications. First, there is a sample job application that has been completed correctly for you to use as a model. Of course, your answers to the questions will be different. Then there is a blank job application for you to complete. Finally there is a worksheet for you to complete and carry with you when you go job hunting. Completing this worksheet ahead of time and taking it with you will give you the information you need when you need it.

Sample Job Application Form

Date of Application _____7-1-02_____ Social Security No. _____123-45-6789_____

Full Name (Last, First) _Yee, Sandra_

Address _6105 Dawn Road_

City _Indianapolis_ State _Indiana_ Zip _46240_

Home Telephone _(317) 555-1010_ Business Telephone _none_

Position Applied For _Bookkeeper_

Referred By _Indianapolis Community College Placement_

When will you be available to begin work? _immediately_

Can you travel if the job requires it? _yes_

Have you been employed here before? _no_ If yes, give date _____

Have you applied for a job here before? _no_ If yes, give date _____

Are you a United States citizen? _yes_

If no, do you have an alien registration card and will you produce it for inspection? _____

If you are a veteran of the U.S. Military Service, give dates of service and branch. _na_

Have you been convicted of a crime in the last seven years? _no_

If Yes, Give Date _na_ Place _na_ Offense _na_

Education:	Name and Address of School	No. of Years Attended	Did You Graduate?	Major/Degree
High School	Ripple HS 855 E. 59 St. Indianapolis	4	yes	Academic
College	Indianapolis Community College 7331 Station St.	2	yes	Accounting
Trade School or Other	none			
Special Training	none			

Employment History (Start with your most recent position)

Name & Address of Employer or Organization	Dates Employed from Month/Year to Month/Year	Nature of Work	Reason for Leaving	Name of Supervisor	Salary
Conn & More Supermarket 420 W. New York St. Indianapolis	9 / 00 5 / 02	Bookkeeper	Part-time while in college	Neal McKinlay	$9.00 per hour
Coalition for the Homeless 4015 E. 32 St. Indianapolis	Summer 99-00	Assisted in inventories of food	Summer volunteer work	Janice Block	na
na					
na					

References (Other than supervisors listed above)

Name	Full Address	Telephone	Relationship
Charles Eckberg	Accounting Department Indianapolis CC 7331 Station St.	555-5990	Professor
Martha Fuller	Physical Educ. Dept. Indianapolis CC 7331 Station St.	555-5991	Professor
Brian Counts	English Department Indianapolis CC 7331 Station St.	555-5994	Professor

Special Skills (foreign languages, licenses, association memberships)

Captain of college fencing team

If you have ever been known by any other name, please indicate.

Sample Job Application Form

Date of Application _____ Social Security No. _____

Full Name (Last, First) _____

Address _____

City _____ State _____ Zip _____

Home Telephone _____ Business Telephone _____

Position Applied For _____

Referred By _____

When will you be available to begin work? _____

Can you travel if the job requires it? _____

Have you been employed here before? _____ If yes, give date _____

Have you applied for a job here before? _____ If yes, give date _____

Are you a United States citizen? _____

If no, do you have an alien registration card and will you produce it for inspection? _____

If you are a veteran of the U.S. Military Service, give dates of service and branch. _____

Have you been convicted of a crime in the last seven years? _____

If Yes, Give Date _____ Place _____ Offense _____

Education:	Name and Address of School	No. of Years Attended	Did You Graduate?	Major/Degree
High School				
College				
Trade School or Other				
Special Training				

Employment History (Start with your most recent position)

Name & Address of Employer or Organization	Dates Employed from Month/Year to Month/Year	Nature of Work	Reason for Leaving	Name of Supervisor	Salary

References (Other than supervisors listed above)

Name	Full Address	Telephone	Relationship

Special Skills (foreign languages, licenses, association memberships)

_____

_____

_____

If you have ever been known by any other name, please indicate.

_____

Job Information Worksheet

Complete the information in this worksheet and tear it out or copy it so that you can carry it with you for reference when you complete job applications.

Name (Use only your legal names, not nicknames)

_____

Other Names You Have Used Legally _____

Address: Building Number & Street _____

_____

City, State, and Zip Code _____

_____

Telephone Number at Home _____

Social Security Number _____

Job Title _____

Date You Are Available _____

Education: High School _____

Dates Attended: From _____ to _____

Type of Diploma _____

Major (if any) _____

Education: College _____

Dates Attended: From _____ to _____

Type of Diploma _____

Major _____

Education: Technical School _____

Dates Attended: From _____ to _____

Type of Diploma _____

Major (if any) _____

Education: Other _____

Dates Attended: From _____ to _____

Type of Diploma _____

Major (if any) _____

Work History (Use this space to include part-time and volunteer work)

Job 1: Name of Company or Organization _____

Address _____

Type of Work _____

Reason for Leaving _____

Dates of Employment _____

Name of Supervisor _____

Job 2: Name of Company or Organization _____

Address _____

Type of Work _____

Reason for Leaving _____

Dates of Employment _____

Name of Supervisor _____

Job 3; Name of Company or Organization _____

Address _____

Type of Work _____

Reason for Leaving _____

Dates of Employment _____

Name of Supervisor _____

Special Skills (List typing wpm, foreign languages, knowledge of computers and software, sports, awards, and any others) _____

_____

_____

Dates of Military Service (if any) _____

References: (Include people who know the strengths an employer might be interested in—teachers, members of the clergy, people you have worked with or for. You can give their business addresses, such as the school they work in. Be sure to ask each person for permission. Do not list relatives such as aunts or cousins.)

Name 1 _____

Business or Organization (if applicable) _____

Street Address _____

City, State, Zip _____

Telephone Number _____

Relationship to You (teacher, friend, colleague, supervisor, etc.) _____

Name 2 _____

Business or Organization (if applicable) _____

Street Address _____

City, State, Zip _____

Telephone Number _____

Relationship to You _____

Name 3 _____

Business or Organization (if applicable) _____

Street Address _____

City, State, Zip _____

Telephone Number _____

Relationship to You _____

Criminal Record (if any) (This includes only convictions—not arrests, youthful offender, or minor traffic violations.)

Date _____

Place _____

Offense _____

Disposition _____

Writing Resumes and Cover Letters

When you answer an ad in a newspaper, you are often asked to send a resume. A resume is a brief statement of your accomplishments. Your goal is to have a winning resume, one that gets you to the next step, the job interview. Every resume must have a cover letter to go with it. The first part of this section explains resumes; the second is about cover letters.

Employers in a variety of industries were asked what recommendations as to resume writing they would give to a young person applying for her or his first job. They offered two major pieces of advice. The first was to be as concise as possible. The second was to be factual and down-to-earth. Some specific suggestions were as follows:

- "List only real achievements. If you have none, write a sincere cover letter stating your goals and your willingness to work hard."

- "Make the resume fit the job. There is no resume that will fit every job."

- "I like to see how well one got through school—interests, honors, energy."

- "If I get a resume of more than two pages from a young person, I'm getting fluff. Either the person can't write or it's baloney."

- "Be honest. Be factual. Avoid exaggeration at all costs."

Since you are looking for your first full-time job, your resume will be brief. You will use it to try to show that you have energy and initiative in whatever you do. Creation of a winning resume, one that gets you an interview, has five steps.

Five steps to a
winning resume

1. Examine the relevant areas of your life in depth, making notes as you go. By writing out the details, you get the material that you need to write a comprehensive, convincing resume. Worksheet spaces are provided in the following pages for you to develop this raw material.

2. Translate the details into the best language for a resume. This language consists of action words, verbs, and vocabulary related to the field of work in which you are job hunting. You can look at the sample resume in this chapter for some examples of this. You can also go to job descriptions in computer-based career information systems or in books to get a feel for the language. If you are in school or working with a counselor, he or she can help you with this.

3. Select the parts of the resume you want and write a rough draft of it.

4. Arrange your resume on the page so that it is easy to read and attractive. You may want to adjust the format several times until it looks the best it can.

5. Proofread your resume. Eliminate all spelling and typographical errors. If you are not good at seeing spelling or usage errors, get help from someone who is. A resume with errors or one that has sloppy corrections or black marks from photocopying will *not* get you an interview. Employers will think that you just don't care about working for them, or if you do care, that you can't tell a good job from a poor one. Be sure to use the spell checker of your word processing program; but remember the checker will only look for words that don't exist. If you type *no* for *on* or *of* instead of *for,* you will not get an error message. So be sure to proofread the final copy again.

The possible sections of a resume are explained in the following resume worksheets. Use the blank spaces after each section to fill in information about yourself. After the worksheets, you will find a good sample resume. Using the worksheet sections and their explanations, decide what should be in your resume. Use the sample resume as a model for layout.

This chapter gives you some information about resume writing. It would be silly to pretend that this is all that can be said about resumes when there are many books on this subject alone. Be sure to consult other books on resume writing if you feel you need more guidance and information. *How to Write a Winning Resume* (VGM Career Books) is a good book to use.

You will note, as you look over the worksheets, that there is no place for your age, marital status, or physical characteristics. That is because it is against the law to include these as factors in job selection. Race, religion, and national origin are other factors that may not be considered. You will want to remember this in your interviews and throughout the job-hunting process. You may also notice that there is no place for a job objective. That belongs in the cover letter, which will be explained in the next part of this chapter. There is also no place for a summary or highlights. The entire resume *is* a summary.

Resume Worksheet 1—The Heading

The heading is an essential section. It must include your name, home address, and telephone number. If you can receive calls at work, include your business number. This makes it easier for people to reach you during the business day.

Name _____

Full Address _____

_____

_____

Telephone Numbers _____

_____

_____

Resume Worksheet 2—Education

Education is also an essential section. Include the degrees you have earned, the institutions at which you earned them, and the dates of attendance. List your most advanced degree first. You should also list any courses taken to upgrade or enhance your skills. Finally, if you were awarded any honors in school, list them. Also include any special course work you took or projects you did. Use these to show unusual accomplishment or energy. Do not list the regular courses of study for your field. The person reading the resume will just see that as an attempt to puff yourself up.

College _____

Dates Attended: From _____ to _____

Type of Diploma _____

Major _____

Special Projects _____

_____

Evidence of Leadership _____

_____

Awards or Honors _____

Technical School _____

Dates Attended: From _____ to _____

Type of Diploma _____

Major _____

Special Projects _____

_____

Evidence of Leadership _____

_____

Awards or Honors _____

High School _____

Dates Attended: From _____ to _____

Type of Diploma _____

Major (if any) _____

Special Projects _____

_____

Evidence of Leadership _____

_____

Awards or Honors _____

Other _____

Dates Attended: From _____ to _____

Type of Diploma _____

Major (if any) _____

Special Projects _____

_____

Evidence of Leadership _____

_____

Awards or Honors _____

Other _____

Dates Attended: From _____ to _____

Type of Diploma _____

Major (if any) _____

Special Projects _____

_____

Evidence of Leadership _____

_____

Awards or Honors _____

Resume Worksheet 3—Work History

Work history should be included if you have held any part-time or summer jobs. They show that you know how to work. It should include each of your jobs, beginning with the most recent. For each job, include the dates you were there, the company, and your title. List your major duties and responsibilities.

Job 1: Name of Company or Organization _____

Address _____

Type of Work _____

Dates of Employment _____

Major Duties and Responsibilities _____

_____

Most Important Accomplishment _____

Job 2: Name of Company or Organization _____

Address _____

Type of Work _____

Dates of Employment _____

Major Duties and Responsibilities _____

_____

Most Important Accomplishment _____

Job 3: Name of Company or Organization _____

Address _____

Type of Work _____

Dates of Employment _____

Major Duties and Responsibilities _____

_____

Most Important Accomplishment _____

Job 4: Name of Company or Organization _____

Address _____

Type of Work _____

Dates of Employment _____

Major Duties and Responsibilities _____

_____

Most Important Accomplishment _____

Resume Worksheet 4—Licenses and Certificates

Professional licenses and certificates is an essential section if these are required for the kind of work you do. Give the title, issuing agency, and date of issuance for each license you hold.

Title of License _____

Issued by _____

Date of Issue _____

Title of License _____

Issued by _____

Date of Issue _____

Title of License _____

Issued by _____

Date of Issue _____

Title of License _____

Issued by _____

Date of Issue _____

Title of License _____

Issued by _____

Date of Issue _____

Resume Worksheet 5—Volunteer Activities

Volunteer activities should be included only if you have activities that show enthusiasm, energy, and a high level of interest. These are characteristics employers like. If your hobbies are only of passing interest to you, do not include this section. When the potential employer starts to talk to you about them in the interview, your lack of real interest will be a strike against you. Use this section to show work that you have done for which you have not been paid or to show hobbies or sports that are really important to you.

Resume Worksheet 6—Special Abilities

Special abilities is an optional section that you should include if you have abilities related to your work, such as a knowledge of foreign languages or computer programming. In general, these are listed after the work history. If you are looking for a job in the computer field, your knowledge of programming languages, computer systems, and software programs should be the first item after the heading.

Sample Resume

Resume

Philip Jamison
571 Vermont Street
Brooklyn, New York 11207
(718) 555-3450

EDUCATION

Albert Einstein High School, Diploma, June 2002
Major: Merchandising
Specialized Courses: Retailing, Fashion Communications, Data Processing, Junior
Achievement Economics, Art Electives in Display and Package Design

WORK EXPERIENCE

2000–present	STOCK CLERK	Blooms Department Store New York, New York

Stock shelves, monitor supplies on the floor to see what is needed, take inventory, assist in unpacking and packing. (Part-time work while in school.)

Summer 1999	MAINTENANCE WORKER	Parks Department New York, New York

Participated in all indoor and outdoor cleanup activities in various parts of Central Park.

OTHER ACTIVITIES

Worked in the school boutique for two years. The school boutique workers are responsible for purchasing merchandise for sale to students, pricing the items, and then working behind the counter selling to students. In the boutique, I moved from being a general worker to being a member of the committee responsible for merchandise selection.

In the Junior Achievement economics class, I worked on a project to select a product and market it. Our group made the largest profit in the class.

SKILLS

Familiar with the IBM PC. Can use data processing and word processing software.
Type 50 WPM.

Now that you have finished your resume, you must prepare a cover letter, which tells employers why you are sending them your resume. Remember that the cover letter is designed to introduce the resume and interest your potential employer in reading your resume, just as the resume is designed to interest that person in meeting you. The cover letter must be neat and clean in both content and production.

Seven sections of the cover letter

1. Your address (unless it is typed on your personal letterhead, which already includes this information).

2. The date.

3. The inside address of the person and company to whom you are sending the resume. If you are addressing a box number in an advertisement include the box number information and the line *To whom it may concern:*.

4. The first paragraph should explain why you are writing this letter. Is it in response to an advertisement, the result of a previous meeting, or at the suggestion of someone who is helping you through your networking contacts?

5. The second paragraph should present one or two highlights of your experience in terms of what you believe to be the requirements of the job or needs of the company.

6. The final paragraph should close with a request for an interview and any pertinent information needed to schedule the interview. This might include hours during which you can be reached at a particular telephone number.

7. Whether the letter is to be sent to a classified ad box or to an individual, the correct closing is, *Sincerely,* or *Yours truly,* followed by your signature, followed by your full name typed out.

The cover letter must always be an individually typed, one-page document on good, 8 1/2" x 11" bond paper. Since the cover letters must be written to particular individuals or at least to particular companies, they cannot be reproduced or photocopied like resumes. Of course, once you have written and rewritten your first cover letter to the point where you really like it and feel it represents you well, you may certainly use the same or similar wording in subsequent letters to other prospective employers. A sample of a good cover letter follows.

Sample Cover Letter

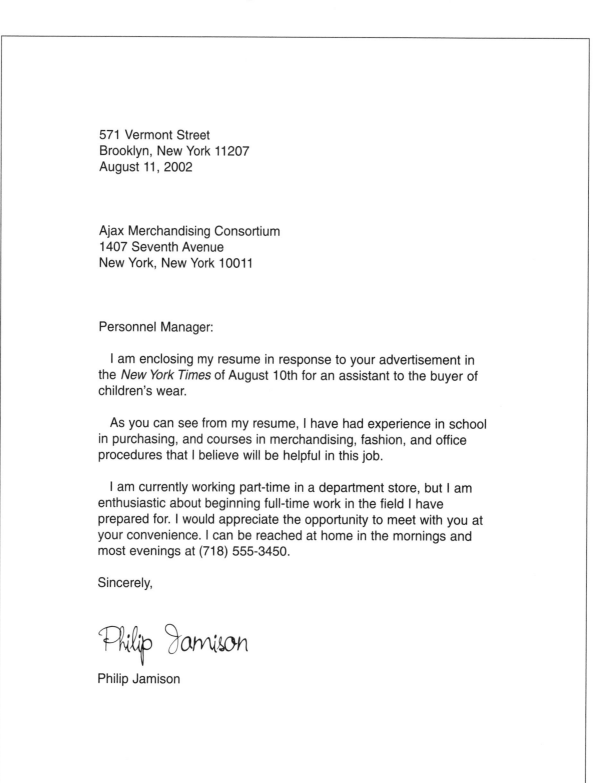

571 Vermont Street
Brooklyn, New York 11207
August 11, 2002

Ajax Merchandising Consortium
1407 Seventh Avenue
New York, New York 10011

Personnel Manager:

 I am enclosing my resume in response to your advertisement in the *New York Times* of August 10th for an assistant to the buyer of children's wear.

 As you can see from my resume, I have had experience in school in purchasing, and courses in merchandising, fashion, and office procedures that I believe will be helpful in this job.

 I am currently working part-time in a department store, but I am enthusiastic about beginning full-time work in the field I have prepared for. I would appreciate the opportunity to meet with you at your convenience. I can be reached at home in the mornings and most evenings at (718) 555-3450.

Sincerely,

Philip Jamison

Philip Jamison

After you have typed your cover letter, proofread it as thoroughly as you did the resume. Handle it carefully to avoid a dirty appearance. Mail the cover letter and resume in an envelope of the appropriate size.

Techno-Tips

Getting the Resume Right

There are four major ways, other than mailing a printed copy, in which you can use technology to submit your resume, and each method calls for somewhat different techniques. For each technique, there is a section within these Techno-Tips.

- You can submit your printed resume by fax directly to an employer or agency working on behalf of the employer. Whether you mail or fax your resume, you may want to assume that it will be scanned into a database for further use. So this section is about creating the scannable resume.

- You can send your resume by E-mail as an attached file. This section is about creating an attached file for submission by E-mail.

- You can respond to Internet ad listings that ask for your resume or resume-type information. This section is about creating the online resume.

- You can create your own Web page to attract prospective employers. This section is, very briefly, about creating a Web page of your own as a way of sending your resume and attracting employers.

Each of the methods of submitting your resume calls for different techniques of layout, general style, and even the choice of words. You will find the details of these techniques in each of the sections that follow.

In addition, each section includes an example of how to change your resume to maximize the utility of the technique. To do this, I have created a sample resume and rewritten it to fit the technology under discussion. You will need to do the same thing. You may very well have several versions of your resume, not just different versions for different employers or jobs, but different versions to take advantage of scanning, E-mail, and resume-listing services.

Creating a Scannable Resume

What is scanning? What should I change to make my resume scannable? What will my scannable resume look like? Depending upon your experience with computers, these are questions you may be asking as you begin reading this section. We begin with some basics, but if you know these, just skip right to the part that tells you what to do.

Scanners are often attached to computers to enter data quickly from print to images that the computer can read. After the image is read into the computer, optical character recognition (OCR) software looks at the image and translates what it sees into letters and numbers. Then other software is used to identify important information about you such as your name and address, your work history, your experience and skills.

OCR software is imperfect, or perhaps, too perfect. When it is looking for perfect matches between the images you have supplied and letters and numbers, it can only translate what it sees against the set of characters it has been given. If it has been given asterisks, for example, and you use bullets to highlight different responsibilities, unlike a human, it cannot think, "Oh yes, this person has used bullets." Instead, it will try to match your bullets against some character, perhaps periods, thereby creating strange sentences indeed. It may not recognize or be able to translate italics or underlining. Parentheses may be misinterpreted as part of the letter they adjoin or as some other symbol. Smudges may become characters and broken letters may be omitted altogether.

Once the resume has been scanned, other software is used to place it in your potential employer's database and then to search it for the key words that the employer has identified for the job you are seeking. While there are a number of different programs for scanning and searching, the rules to increase your chances are generally the same.

The rules for creating a scannable resume, then, are fairly simple. In fact, that is the rule: KEEP IT SIMPLE. Here are ten pointers to show you *how to write a winning scannable resume.*

1. Use white, 8½" × 11" paper, printed on one side only.

2. Use a standard font such as Arial, Optima, Universe, Times New Roman, or Courier in 12-point typeface. Do not condense or expand the type.

3. Avoid all "fancy" type—no italics, underlining, boxes, graphics, bullets, or columns. Do use capital letters and line spacing to help organize your resume.

4. Be sure to put each of the following on separate lines: name, address, phone number, fax number, and E-mail address. Put your name only at the top of each additional page.

5. Use a structured resume format with clear headings such as those suggested throughout this book.

6. Increase your use of key words, particularly nouns and industry jargon, to increase your chances that the key word search will select your resume.

7. Be sure to print your resume on a laser or ink jet printer. Dot matrix print and less than perfect photo copies do not scan well.

8. Do not staple or fold your resume. Either of these can make marks that will "confuse" the OCR software. Mail it in a large enough, protective envelope.

9. Faxing often reduces the quality of an image. If you must fax your resume, set the fax machine on "fine" rather than "standard" mode, and, if possible, follow with a mailed copy.

10. If you are uncertain whether your resume will be scanned or read, ask the employer. If you cannot do that, you may want to send two copies with Post-It Notes attached, identifying one as the "scannable resume" and the other as the "hard copy resume."

Sample Scannable Resume

Jose Emanuel
1800 N. Dodge
Omaha, NE 68130
401 555-7749
emanuel@xyz.edu

OBJECTIVE
Drafter for public and large private design and construction

EXPERIENCE
Part-Time Drafter's Assistant, Quewit Manufacturers, Omaha, Nebraska, 2001 to present
Assisted in projects for a library and a shopping mall

EDUCATION
Technical Community College, Bellevue, Nebraska, enrolled in evening computer-aided design program. Expect AAS in 2002.
North High School, Omaha, Nebraska, 1997–2000

INTERESTS
Team sports, mountain climbing, photography

SKILLS
Accuracy, analytical ability, team member, high energy, problem solving

Sending Your Resume by E-Mail

You may want to send your resume by E-mail because that is what you have been requested to do by the employer whose ad you are answering. You may have found that ad in one of the traditional sources, such as the newspaper, or by going to the Web home page of companies that interest you. More and more companies, particularly those in the high-tech field, list job openings right on their own websites.

If you use E-mail, you probably are aware of the limited ability you have to format the material you are sending. In addition, depending upon the program the other party has, the E-mail may arrive with even less style than you included. Although communication by E-mail across the Internet improves almost day by day, it is still difficult for you to know how well the page you send will resemble the page your potential employer receives. Very often, the first page of your E-mail is taken up by the header that contains a raft of information about the machine-to-machine transmission of your letter. If you send your resume by E-mail, the only thing the employer may receive on the first screen will be your name. In addition, employers who want to print your resume or store it in a database, must find where it begins and separate that from the unneeded header.

You can exercise some control over the appearance of your E-mailed resume by sending it as an attached file to your E-mail rather than as a part of the E-mail itself. Because you have no way of knowing which word processing program your potential employer has, the best way to ensure compatibility of sending and receiving is to send your resume as an ASCII file. ASCII (pronounced *askee*) is a simple form of text recognized by virtually all computer platforms (for example, both Windows and Macintosh) and all computer applications of interest to us. ASCII stands for American Standard Code for Information Interchange.

Without getting into technicalities of binary coding, we can explain that one of the reasons that ASCII works is because it is used to communicate in text that has no frills and virtually no formatting. Remember the rule for scannable resumes was KEEP IT SIMPLE. Well, the rule for ASCII text is KEEP IT SIMPLER. You can use all of the resume ideas you used in developing your scannable resume with a few additional pointers. Here are the ten pointers to show you *how to write a winning E-mailed resume.*

1. Use a standard font such as Arial, Optima, Universe, Times New Roman, or Courier in 12-point typeface. Do not condense or expand the type.

2. Avoid all "fancy" type—no italics, underlining, boxes, graphics, bullets, or columns. Do use capital letters and line spacing to help organize your resume.

3. Do not use any centering. Keep all text left-justified, straight on the left margin.

4. The computer programs that will read your resume prefer simple left-justified text. However, if you want to indent, do not use a tab key; just type in the number of spaces you want.

5. Be sure to put each of the following on separate lines: name, address, phone number, fax number, and E-mail address. Put your name only at the top of each additional page.

6. Use a structured resume format with clear headings such as those suggested throughout this book.

7. Increase your use of key words, particularly nouns and industry jargon, to increase your chances that the key word search will select your resume.

8. Before you send your resume, save it in "text only" mode. On most programs, this is called, "rich text format" or RTF. Often, you will have to save your resume file and close it before you can attach it to an E-mail message.

9. Of course, you will not be printing your resume and sending it. You will be transmitting it by E-mail, so you need not worry about paper and print quality. However, you should print a copy of your resume to see what it looks life *before* you send it.

You have read about proofreading and checking your resume. All of that should be done *before* you hit the fateful send button.

10. Then, when you are sending your E-mail response, direct the attention of the reader to the attached file. Be sure to find out how to attach a file in the E-mail program you are using. In most cases, there is a button or pull-down menu within E-mail that lets you attach a file. Once you find and activate it, the program prompts you for the name and location of the file you are using. For example, in the version of Eudora that I use, within the Message menu there is a command to "Attach File." Once I click on that, the directory of all my files comes on the screen. I scroll through the directories and subdirectories to find the file I want to attach, click on it, and the job is done. Hit the "send" button and your resume is gone. So be sure you are ready to send it before you do so.

For examples of how to set up ASCII or RTF, look at the resume in the "scannable resume" section. Just left-justify the headings instead of centering them and you have a resume you can save in RTF. You may also want to create a more traditional, print version of your resume to bring with you when you go for the job interview.

Using a Web-Based Resume-Listing Service

In one of the Techno-Tips in the last chapter, you learned that there are a number of Internet sites that list job openings. These included the following: careermosaic.com, hotjobs.com, careerpath.com, and mon ster.com. These databases are subscribed to by employers who list openings and look for responses from potential employees. In one sense, you can look at using these lists of job openings as the same as using ads in a newspaper or magazine to find jobs. However, in another sense, these lists are quite different because you can often respond to the ad right online. In some cases, you can submit a resume that you have developed on your word processor. In other cases, you will be asked to fill in a profile using a structured form.

Here are some tips for submitting your resume over the Internet through one of the database companies mentioned above. You will need to be brief and to the point, stress skills, and work within a framework provided by the database organizer. Often there will be a form to complete that asks you to use the "carriage return" or "enter" key as you enter information. That is because you are using ASCII format, a kind of standardized computer communication language, and you want to be sure to stay within the vertical and horizontal sides of the box provided.

A word of caution. Some people prefer not to put home addresses and telephone numbers on the Web. Remember, just as you can get to the site to list your resume and look at those of others, so can others get to your resume. Once you have put your address and telephone number on the Web, there's no way to recall the information. Some people will list their city, state, and E-mail address. Some prefer to list only their E-mail address and to include the location of the work they are seeking in the objective box. On the other hand, some resume-listing services require your address to be sure that you are on the up and up. If you do list any identifying information, be sure that you are cautious in setting up any meetings or giving any further information in response to queries. I am not suggesting that you hide. I am suggesting that you verify any further requests for information to be sure they are coming from a potential employer and not a prankster.

Following is an example of a resume-listing form completed for the sample resume of Jose Emanuel. You will see that some information that was in the resume has no place in the form and that other information, such as dates of employment, needs to be supplied in greater detail.

Sample Resume-Listing Form

Name Jose Emanuel

Home Address 1800 N. Dodge

City Omaha   **State** NE   **Zip** 68130

Work Address

City   **State**   **Zip**

Home Phone Number 401-555-7749

Work Phone Number

Fax Number

E-Mail Address emanuel@xyz.edu

OBJECTIVE (Type of Employment Sought)
Drafter for public and large private design and construction

EDUCATION (Post–High School Only)
School Technical Community College   **Major** Computer-Aided Design

Degree AAS   **Year of Graduation**   2002   **GPA** 3.2

School   **Major**

Degree   **Year of Graduation**   **GPA**

School   **Major**

Degree   **Year of Graduation**   **GPA**

School   **Major**

Degree   **Year of Graduation**   **GPA**

EMPLOYMENT HISTORY

Employer Quewit Manufacturers

Job Title Drafter's Assistant

From (mm/yy) 7/01   **To (mm/yy) [you would enter current date]**

Description of Duties
Assisted in projects for a library and shopping mall

Employer

Job Title

From (mm/yy)   **To (mm/yy)**

Description of Duties

ADDITIONAL INFORMATION (skills, abilities, etc.)
Accuracy, analytical ability, team member high energy, problem solving

---

A Few Words on Your Web Page Resume

You can use the most sophisticated tools of the Internet including multimedia and links to other parts of the Web to create your own Web page as an advertisement for your services. The techniques for creating such a Web page are beyond the scope of this book, but if you are even considering doing this, you probably have some of the skills necessary. However, a word or two of caution so that you know how to create a winning Web-page resume.

1. Remember the purpose of the resume is to get you a job interview. Restrict your information to that which serves the purpose.

2. Consider that if you send your readers off on links to other parts of the World Wide Web, you may never see them again. Consider how any links contribute to *your* getting a job.

3. Be sure to make your information accessible. Consider how a potential employer will know that your website is out there advertising your services.

4. Do not include every graphic or auditory feature you can dream up. Do include those that demonstrate that you are the best person for the job you are seeking.

Taking Tests to Get a Job

You may have hoped that once you were out of school you would never have to take a test again. However, many jobs require tests as part of their application procedures. Almost all civil service jobs require tests. In addition, many secretarial or office jobs require tests of typing or clerical abilities. It is impossible to predict whether or not a particular employer is going to ask you to take a test, but you can be prepared. This section will give you some ways to do that.

First, be aware that tests can take several forms. You can be asked to answer questions in writing or by filling in answer blanks. You may be asked to perform some task, such as typing a document. You may be asked in an interview situation to talk about what you would do in particular circumstances. Whatever the type of test, it will be related to the job you will be performing. Therefore, if you are prepared for the job, you will pass the test.

Most civil service jobs require tests. You can study for these ahead of time by getting books that describe the tests and give sample questions and answers. One book, for example, is *The Civil Service Handbook* (ARCO). ARCO is a company that publishes many of these kinds of books. There is probably at least one book for every type of test given. Of course, it is difficult to prepare well at the last minute. So if you are considering a civil service job, get the appropriate book and begin work as soon as you can.

If you are applying for jobs that require skills such as typing or driving, expect to be tested. Practice before you go to the employer so you are prepared to be tested.

Whenever you go for a test for a job, whether the job is in civil service or business, follow these simple hints.

Five hints for test taking

1. Learn all you can about the test before you go to take it.

2. Study from test preparation books or practice your skills.

3. Know what tools you need for the test, and bring them with you. This *always* includes at least four sharpened pencils and two pens with blue or black ink.

4. Know the time you are supposed to be at the test and the location. Be sure you know how to travel to the location. Get there about twenty minutes earlier than you are scheduled to.

5. Get a good night's sleep before the test, and eat a solid breakfast on the day of the test.

When an organization is considering offering you a job, they may ask you to take a physical exam or a drug-use test or a polygraph (lie detector) test. It is your right to refuse to take the test. However, you can be pretty sure that you will not get the job if you do not take the test.

Additional Papers for Your Job Search

In addition to the papers already identified—the application, the resume, the cover letter, and tests—you will need some personal papers during your job search. Some employers will ask for these during the application process. Others may want them as soon as you are hired. It is a good idea to have these ready as soon as you begin job hunting.

Your *Social Security card* is your ticket to work in the United States. You cannot be employed without one. To get a Social Security card, go to any district office of the Social Security Administration. Bring a copy of your birth or baptismal certificate to attach to the application. It will take six to eight weeks to get a card, so apply for one right away. Once you have a card, put one copy away in a safe place and keep the other with your job application worksheet information. You will often need your Social Security number, so write it in several places that you can get to easily.

A *Selective Service Registration Acknowledgment* form may be required of you if you are male. The law requires that all men register within one month of their eighteenth birthday. You can register at your local United States Post Office. If you have finished military service, you should have your discharge papers.

High school or college diplomas and *copies of your current transcripts or grade reports* may be asked for to prove the statements on your application and to show your grades. Have copies of these ready, and take them with you.

Your *birth certificate* or *baptismal certificate* may be required to prove your age and citizenship.

Citizenship papers, an *alien registration receipt card,* often called a *Green Card,* or other appropriate proof of your right to work in the United States should be available if you were not born a United States citizen.

A *work permit* should be carried if you are under eighteen years of age. You can find out the particular requirements in your state from a local state employment service office.

A *union card,* if you have one, should be carried.

A *portfolio* of your work, if you are in an art-related field, is also appropriate.

The *job application worksheets* with your information should be on hand whenever you go to apply for a job so that you are not caught not knowing enough about yourself.

A *resume*, if you have prepared one, should be carried so that you can leave it as a reminder to people you have met.

As you look over the list of papers, you will see that you want to carry some with you as you go to employers and that you will want to have others ready at home. If you have a briefcase, carry the papers in a folder or envelope inside the case. If you prefer not to carry a briefcase, get a sturdy manila envelope that will hold all of your papers. Remember to carry sharpened pencils and a pen with blue or black ink with you all the time.

Now that you have finished working on your papers, you are ready to move to the next step: job interviews.

Summary Worksheet

In this chapter, you learned how to prepare the papers for a job search. Use the checklist that follows to be sure you have covered all bases.

_____ I have a Social Security card.

_____ I know what to expect to see on a job application.

_____ I have prepared my personal information to complete a job application.

_____ I know the six tips for completing a job application.

_____ I have prepared my resume.

_____ I have proofread my resume and there are no mistakes.

_____ I have proofread my resume *again* and I am sure there are no mistakes.

_____ I know what to include in a cover letter with my resume.

_____ I know how to send a scannable resume by fax.

_____ I know how to submit my resume online.

_____ I am ready to take the appropriate tests for the job I want.

_____ I have gone over the list of suggested items to carry on a job search.

_____ I know which ones to carry all the time and which ones to have ready at home.

_____ I am ready to think about job interviews.

People—Seven Steps to a Winning Interview 4

Once you have identified some places to look for a job and you have begun filling out applications and sending resumes, you can expect to be called for interviews. This chapter will take you through the seven steps to a winning interview, an interview that gets you the job you want. This does not mean you will get the first job for which you are interviewed. Most people go through many interviews before they get the right job. Many of them report, however, that they get better and better at it with practice.

The research for this chapter included discussions with employers in a variety of industries including advertising, accounting, banking, merchandising, and computers. They stressed the importance of preparing for an interview so that you can present your skills and experiences in a way that has meaning for the employer. These seven steps will help you do that.

It is important to remember that an interview is not a contest between you and the employer. A winning interview means that you both end up on the same team. Listed below are the seven steps that will put you on the winning team. The rest of the chapter gives you more information on how to carry out each of the steps and provides you with worksheets that will help you prepare for your interview.

Seven steps to a winning interview

> 1. Get all the preliminary information you need when you make the appointment for an interview.
>
> 2. Assess your own strengths and weaknesses.
>
> 3. Learn all that you can about the job and the company or organization.
>
> 4. Think about how your skills fit the job.
>
> 5. Plan how you will look as carefully as you plan what to say.
>
> 6. Accept your nervousness, and turn nervous energy into positive energy.
>
> 7. Know the kinds of questions you will probably be asked and how to answer them.

Making the Interview Appointment

You are now at the stage where you are ready to make arrangements. This means you have developed enough interest in a potential employer so that he or she is willing to spend some time with you. You may have done this through networking contacts, through referral by an employment service of one type or another, or by writing in answer to an advertisement or some other type of lead.

Generally speaking, you will receive a telephone call from a member of the personnel department or from a secretary representing the person who will interview you. Sometimes you will get a letter asking you to telephone, and sometimes you will get a letter asking you to come at a specific time. Sometimes you are the one who makes the first telephone call if you are answering a newspaper advertisement that says to call rather than to write.

As soon as you send out your first resume or make your first contact, you should be ready to accept the invitation to an interview. To do this, you need to think about the information you will need so that you will be in the right place at the right time, prepared to do your best. Listed below are the eight items of information you need.

Eight items of information you need before the interview

1. The name of the company

2. The street address of the company

3. Travel directions

4. The name of the person you are going to see

5. The room number of that person

6. The date and time of the interview

7. The name of the person to whom you are speaking

8. The telephone number of that person

In many cases, the person who will interview you is not part of a personnel department, and the secretary calling you is not particularly familiar with making arrangements for an employment interview. You must take the responsibility for getting the information you need.

It is often so exciting when the call for an interview comes that it is difficult to remember all your needs during the call. But you must! Keep the following Interview Arrangements Worksheets handy, and use them when you get the call. Make more copies if you need them. If you might get some calls at work and some at home, keep copies in both places. Be sure you have all the spellings and pronunciations correct before you hang up. Remember, it is better to ask to have something repeated than to go into the interview addressing Mr. Baily as "Mr. Quail."

Notice that the Interview Arrangements Worksheets end with a place for results and follow-up. Save these worksheets to keep track of the developments in your job hunt.

Interview Arrangements Worksheet 1

Name of Organization _____

Street Address _____

Room Number _____

Date _____

Travel Directions _____

_____

_____

Name of Interviewer _____

_____

Title of Interviewer _____

Person Making Arrangements _____

Telephone Number _____

Materials to Bring _____

_____

Additional Notes _____

_____

_____

_____

Other People I Met _____

_____

_____

_____

Results of Interview _____

_____

_____

Next Steps _____

_____

_____

Interview Arrangements Worksheet 2

Name of Organization _____

Street Address _____

Room Number _____

Date _____

Travel Directions _____

_____

_____

Name of Interviewer _____

_____

Title of Interviewer _____

Person Making Arrangements _____

Telephone Number _____

Materials to Bring _____

_____

Additional Notes _____

_____

_____

_____

Other People I Met _____

_____

_____

_____

Results of Interview _____

_____

_____

Next Steps _____

_____

_____

Interview Arrangements Worksheet 3

Name of Organization _____

Street Address _____

Room Number _____

Date _____

Travel Directions _____

_____

_____

Name of Interviewer _____

_____

Title of Interviewer _____

Person Making Arrangements _____

Telephone Number _____

Materials to Bring _____

_____

Additional Notes _____

_____

_____

_____

Other People I Met _____

_____

_____

_____

Results of Interview _____

_____

_____

Next Steps _____

_____

_____

Interview Arrangements Worksheet 4

Name of Organization _____

Street Address _____

Room Number _____

Date _____

Travel Directions _____

_____

_____

Name of Interviewer _____

_____

Title of Interviewer _____

Person Making Arrangements _____

Telephone Number _____

Materials to Bring _____

_____

Additional Notes _____

_____

_____

_____

Other People I Met _____

_____

_____

_____

Results of Interview _____

_____

_____

Next Steps _____

_____

_____

Assessing Your Strengths and Weaknesses

Before you can go into an interview and let someone else know what your strengths are and how you can overcome any weaknesses that you have, you have to understand these things yourself. Just as you had to think about a lot of information to prepare your resume, you need to do this before the job interview. Once you have done this, you will be ready to think about the skills that are needed on the job you are seeking and how to match your skills to those needed.

There are three worksheets on the pages that follow. The first one asks you to think of skills you have developed in various activities in your life. Remember, you may be looking for your first full-time, paid job, but you have been working for a long time. You have worked in school. You may have worked at a part-time job. Perhaps you worked in community or volunteer activities. Think also of jobs you have done for your own family, even though you may not have been paid for them. The second worksheet gives a list of traits that employers said they found important. You are asked to think of whether you have these traits and what examples you have from any area of your life. The last worksheet in this section asks you to assess honestly any weaknesses you have and how you can overcome them. In all of this, try to think of strengths and weaknesses as they relate to the kind of job you wish to find.

Strength Assessment Worksheet 1

I have acquired the following job skills in school:

Skill
EXAMPLE: <u>Know word processing</u>

Program, Course, or Other Source
<u>Took word processing 1 and 2</u>

_____

_____

_____

_____

_____

_____

_____

_____

_____

_____

I have acquired the following job skills in part-time work:

Skill
EXAMPLE: <u>Patience</u>

Job Responsibility
<u>Cleaning up in the park</u>

_____

_____

_____

_____

_____

_____

_____

_____

I have acquired the following job skills in volunteer, leisure, or family activities:

Skill
EXAMPLE: <u>Persuasion</u>

Activity
<u>I collected funds for the Red Cross</u>

_____

_____

_____

_____

_____

_____

_____

_____

Strength Assessment Worksheet 2

Listed below are ten traits. Put a check next to each one that is true of you, and describe how you used each trait in some work, school, or other activity.

Trait   **Activity**

_____ Teamworker   _____

                                             _____

                                             _____

_____ Tactful   _____

                                             _____

                                             _____

_____ Able to change   _____

                                             _____

                                             _____

_____ Able to start things on my own   _____

                                             _____

                                             _____

_____ Self-disciplined   _____

                                             _____

                                             _____

_____ Follow through on work   _____

                                             _____

                                             _____

_____ Hard worker   _____

                                             _____

                                             _____

_____ Honest and sincere   _____

                                             _____

                                             _____

_____ Able to think clearly under pressure _____

                                             _____

                                             _____

_____ Get along well with others   _____

                                             _____

                                             _____

Strength Assessment Worksheet 3

What do you consider your three greatest weaknesses and how are you working to overcome them? (Knowing your weaknesses, not pretending you are Superman or Wonder Woman, helps you identify your strengths.)

Weakness

I am overcoming it by:

EXAMPLE: <u>Losing my temper</u>

<u>Learning to count slowly to ten</u>

1._____

_____

_____

_____

_____

_____

_____

_____

2._____

_____

_____

_____

_____

_____

_____

_____

3._____

_____

_____

_____

_____

_____

_____

Learning About the Job

Before you go for a job interview, you need to be able to look at things from an employer's point of view. Looking at things from the employer's point of view will help you answer questions so that your answers are meaningful to her or to him. When you are in school, you are often called on to answer questions with right answers, answers that center on you. In the job interview, the right answer always centers on the job and how you relate to it.

If you are using any of the employment services discussed in Chapter 2, you can receive help from the counselors in getting information about the jobs you are applying for and about the company or organizations that are offering these jobs. You can also use the general sources in the library that have been mentioned—computer-based career information delivery systems and printed information that describes jobs in general. If you know anyone who is in a similar job or who works for the company to which you will be applying, talk to that person for information.

The following job information worksheet gives you an idea of the kinds of questions you will want to know about each job. You may want to duplicate the worksheet before you fill it in because you will probably apply for more than one job before you are offered a job that you accept.

Techno-Tips

Preparing for the Interview

Earlier you learned about using the Internet to get information about jobs and occupations in general so that you could begin thinking about the conditions of work and the kind of job setting you want. Now it is time to return to the same Internet sources to see how useful they are once you know you will be interviewed by a particular company.

Here are some of the sources that we have already identified for job information. You can go to resume-listing sites for job advertisements. These sites include careermosaic.com, hotjobs.com, careerpath.com, jobtrak.com, and monster.com. The job listings on the sites often give details of what the employer wants in the employee. Take these as signposts on the way to a winning job interview. The more specific the information provided, the better you can use it in preparing for a job interview.

Go to the website of the organization for which you will interview. Once there, look at the listing for your job, if posted, but look beyond the listings. Look for publicity releases and news items. These often give clues to directions the company plans to take or to problems they have solved. Look at mission statements or other general information. All of these are clues to what the company hopes to accomplish. All of them are also clues as to what you can stress about the match between your background and the organization's needs.

Use online indexes to newspapers such as the *New York Times*, the *San Jose Mercury News*, and others to search for articles about the organization. Remember the company's website will have only the information the company chose to put there. News articles may present more objective information, both favorable and unfavorable information, and information about changes in the organization that the company did not care to include on its website. Look for information about the industry as a whole and the company's competitors as well. The more prepared you are with information, the better you can respond to the questions you will be asked.

Use online news groups to get the unofficial news, the "virtual water cooler gossip" about organizations. Because there are no organizational filters on the information, the material in news groups may be more or less accurate than information in other sources. You will need to exercise more caution in using the news group information. However, you can look at the identity of the person who posted the information, remembering that that information may be fake as well. DejaNews (dejanews.com) is an excellent search engine for new groups, and it also provides profiles of the sender authors.

Remember, your purpose in searching these sources is to get information about the company so that you can match your skills and knowledge to their needs. It is important that you show you know the organization without coming across as a "know-it-all."

If you are preparing for an Internet interview, the suggestions for research are the same as for an in-person interview. On its website, VIEWnet posted responses to a survey of employers who had conducted interviews using its service. One wrote: "Many students did not have much knowledge about us. Students should be coached by the schools to research the employers and be prepared as if [the Internet interview] were an on-site interview."

Job Information Worksheet

1. What is the major product or service of this organization?

_____

_____

2. How does the job I am seeking contribute to this product or service?

_____

_____

_____

3. What are the major responsibilities of the job I am seeking?

_____

_____

_____

4. What skills or knowledge does someone need to carry out these responsibilities?

_____

_____

_____

_____

_____

5. Which of these skills or knowledge do I have?

_____

_____

_____

_____

_____

Matching Your Skills to the Job

If you filled in the Job Information Worksheet, you have already begun to think about how your skills and knowledge fit the job you are seeking. In the worksheet that follows, you will bring together what you have learned about yourself and about the job.

Bringing these together and concentrating on them when giving your answers will produce a winning interview. Sometimes employers ask general questions, like "Tell me about yourself." They really want to know about you in relation to their job. This is an opportunity to take information from the Job Match Worksheet that follows and talk about it. You will be able to say something like, "I understand that one of the major responsibilities of this job is delivering materials to many building sites around town. I really know this town well and can get around easily. I took driver's education courses, and I am a careful driver. I have never had any traffic violations."

Job Match Worksheet

Job Requirement	**My Qualifications**	**Proof**
Example: Able to handle and keep track of cash	Trustworthy Used to dealing with money	Treasurer of Junior Baseball League

Planning for a Good First Impression

Like it or not, the first impression anyone has of you is a visual one. You want to use that to your advantage so that your appearance makes the interviewer, your potential employer, want to listen to you.

All of the employers questioned about interviews said pretty much the same thing. They want to see someone who is neat and clean and whose appearance shows that they know what the working world expects. There are some definite things you can do to create the appearance of caring about the job and knowing your way in business.

An employer simply will not want to hire someone to take care of a job who has not learned to take care of herself or himself. Here are some good grooming tips.

Hair care tips

Your hair should be neatly and attractively cut. If you have a problem with dandruff, ask your pharmacist to help you select a special shampoo.

Teeth tips

Clean teeth are the result of ongoing good dental care. If you don't have clean teeth, you probably have bad breath. If you have bad breath, interviewers will spend their time turning away from you rather than listening to you. See your dentist to be sure your teeth are in good condition. Floss and brush your teeth twice a day. Be sure to brush your teeth right before going for an interview.

Bad breath can also be caused by eating a lot of garlic or onions. Some people hold on to these odors for a long time. Your best bet is not to eat dishes with garlic or onions the day before an interview.

If you are not sure of your breath, put a mint in your mouth just before the interview, but be sure to finish it or throw it away before you get into the office. All of the employers said that chewing gum or eating candy during the interview was one of the fastest ways *not* to get hired.

Hand tips

Be sure that your hands are clean and your nails are well manicured. This does not mean you have to use polish. Just be sure your nails are clipped evenly, the cuticles are trimmed, and there is no dirt under the nails.

Since it is your goal to attract the interviewer to your ideas, not your hands, it is a good idea, if you are a woman, to wear only clear or very light polish.

Body tips   Be sure to shower or bathe the day of an interview. Use deodorant. If you have particularly heavy perspiration, use an antiperspirant.

Clothing tips   Select clothing that shows you know you are in a business situation. Ask yourself this question: Do people who hold jobs like the one I want usually wear suits to work?

If the answer is "yes" and you are a man, wear a suit with a shirt and tie to the interview. Your shoes should be similarly formal in style. Do not wear sneakers or casual moccasins with a suit.

If the answer is "yes" and you are a woman, then you should wear a tailored suit, blouse, and dress shoes.

If the answer is "no, people would not usually wear suits to this job," you have a little more freedom in what you wear. However, remember, it is always better to be more conservative when you go for a job interview. A man can wear neatly pressed slacks with a sport jacket or sweater. If you are a woman, you can wear a skirt and blouse or a tailored dress.

The clothes you wear should also make you feel good about yourself. Sometimes it is the color of clothes that gives us a special feeling. Sometimes it is the way they fit. Try to choose clothes that make you feel good or cheerful.

Be sure your clothes have been freshly laundered or dry cleaned for each interview. There will be no chance then of spots or of lingering body odor.

Accessory tips   The key word in accessories is moderation. Remember, you want to draw attention to your thoughts, not your earrings. If you want to wear jewelry, keep it small and simple. If you wear scent—perfume or after-shave lotion—keep it light.

Accepting and Using Nervousness

A number of people who were recently hired were asked about their experiences in the job interview process. Every single one of them said that he or she was nervous. However, each of them had also found a way to use the nervous energy or to control it.

Here are some of the answers that the successful job applicants gave.

- "I know I need rest. I need to relax physically. The day before an interview, I didn't run around shopping. I went home, read the paper, and got a good night's sleep."

- "I just focus on getting there. Then I walk to the interview. That gets rid of a lot of tension."

- "I go through a lot of normal stuff like before a test. I try to plan the interview in my mind, think of the questions I might be asked. Also dressing well makes me feel confident."

- "I rely on thinking of the actor's saying. It's something like, 'If you're nervous before you go onstage, you won't be nervous onstage and if you're not nervous before you go onstage, you're in trouble.' I really just let the nervousness happen. All the nervousness beforehand gets you prepared, psyched."

- "I use a little meditation and visualization. I picture myself being calm and having an easy flowing conversation with another human being."

You may have some ways you already use to help yourself in tension-producing situations. If you want more information about how to use these techniques specifically for interviews as well as more information on all of the interview preparation steps, read *How to Have a Winning Job Interview* (VGM Career Books).

Answering the Questions

If you think ahead of time about the kinds of questions you will be asked, it is easier to be prepared with the answers you want to give. There are three basic kinds of questions employers will ask.

Three types of interview questions

1. *The specific question*—some examples are:
   - What were your major courses of study?
   - Why did you choose those courses?
   - What was the most important thing you learned in school?
   - Do you plan to continue your education?
   - Do you feel your education was worthwhile?
   - What did you learn in _____ (some experience on your resume or application)?
   - (After a description of the job) How do you see yourself fitting in with this job?

2. *The general question*—some examples are:
   - Tell me about yourself.
   - Why do you think you are the best person for this job?
   - Why do you want this job?
   - Is there anything else about you that you would like me to know?

3. *The problem question*—in this type of question, the employer describes a situation that you might come across on the job and asks you how you would handle it.

To answer a *specific question*, be specific. Suppose you were asked, "What was your most important course in school?" Do not answer, "Lunch." Do not answer "Gym," unless you are applying for a job in recreation. Answer with the name of a course or several courses related to the job you are seeking. Explain why this course was important to you then and now. Here is a good answer:

The most important course I took was "Introduction to Word Processing." It really helped me see how computers can be used not only to type letters but to make office work more efficient in so many ways.

General questions are harder to answer. Interviewers often use general questions to see what you will choose to say.

When asked a general question, you have to make a series of quick choices. First, you have to decide whether to answer the question or whether to ask a question about it. If the interviewer asks, for example, "Tell me about your background," you can ask, "Would you like me to start with my education or my work experience?" On the other hand, you can use that opportunity to point out your strengths, knowledge of the job, and information about the company.

As soon as you have made the choice to answer the question, you have to decide where to begin. As often as possible, try to use general questions to give the information you decided you wanted to communicate in your analysis of strengths. Of course, if a question is really vague and you have no idea what the interviewer means, ask for clarification.

When you are asked a *problem-solving question*, the first thing to do is think. Don't be afraid to take some time to plan your answer. The interviewer will respect you more. Try to hear the entire problem when it is first presented, but if it is complicated and you have missed some part, ask to have it repeated.

Answer as if you are already on the job. Don't speak as if you are a student but as if you are already a worker. Remember that you will be part of an organization. One of the key questions in the interviewer's mind is: "Do I want this person on my team?" While you do not want to go running to your boss too quickly, you also do not want to seem to be taking on the whole world by yourself.

Remember your strengths that you identified on the worksheets in this chapter. Remember how they match the skills and knowledge this job requires. Use that information in answering any type of question.

You also identified weaknesses on your worksheets. Understanding your own weaknesses will help you with your answers when one of them is brought up in an interview. It is important that you be honest about your background, but do not make it seem worse than it really is. Suppose you dropped out of high school, have just completed your equivalency diploma, and are now in a job interview. You do not have to walk in and say, "I dropped out of high school for three years. That's it. Take it or leave it." However, if the interviewer asks about your education, you can say something like the following:

I have just completed my equivalency diploma. Maybe I should have stayed in high school, but it wasn't right for me at the time. As I got older and smarter, I realized I did need more education. In fact, now that I have my diploma, I am planning to take some courses at the community college at night.

Questions you need not answer

Federal and state laws prohibit employers from asking certain questions unless they are directly related to the job for which you are being interviewed. The areas of your life about which you cannot be questioned include the following:

Questions about your race, religion, or ethnic origin

Questions about your marital status or children

Questions about your age, height, weight, health, or handicapping conditions

Questions about whom you date or live with or about your friends

You are permitted by law to answer these questions, but the employer is not allowed to ask them. Before you decide to answer them, think about how you would feel working for an employer who asks these kinds of questions. You may think the employer is asking them because he or she does not know they are illegal. However, so much has been written about them that it is hard to believe an employer would not know the rules.

You may decide to answer briefly and then say, "I think there are more important things about me that relate to this job. I would rather talk about them." Of course, if you refuse to answer, you might not get the job. This in itself is discrimination. If you think you have been discriminated against on an illegal basis, you can file a complaint with the Equal Employment Opportunity Commission (EEOC) in Washington, DC. You can contact the Fair Employment Practices Commission in your own state and decide whether filing a complaint with them is appropriate. And you can also sue the company, using your own attorney.

Of course, you should not go into an interview expecting to be asked inappropriate questions. Most employers are familiar with the laws and abide by them. If you begin with suspicions, you may divert yourself from your real purpose—getting a job.

Listening—
a Special Tip

Listening is the key to winning answers and to a winning interview. You let people know you are listening to them by facing them and by maintaining eye contact.

One of the most important reasons for listening to the interviewer is so that you can hear the question. People who don't listen, who are jumping ahead in their minds to answer questions they have not yet heard, do not do well in interviews. Not only do they fail to provide the information requested, but they come across as poor communicators, as being "out of it."

A major part of listening is not interrupting. Sometimes it is hard to tell if the interviewer has finished speaking or is just pausing to gather thoughts or breathe. Generally speaking, you can tell by watching the person. If the interviewer turns to you or looks at you, a response is probably called for. On the other hand, if the interviewer is looking into the distance or down at the desk, it is probably just a pause in speech.

Remember that one of *The 7 Habits of Highly Effective People* is to "seek first to understand, then to be understood." Good listening is the secret of understanding.

Techno-Tips

Internet Interviewing

A few companies are now making use of the Internet or video conferencing to interview people at distant locations. If you are going to be interviewed through use of the Internet or video conferencing, all of the suggestions in this chapter apply, but there are some special considerations.

All of the suggestions on good grooming apply. However, you must remember that you will probably only be seen from the chest up, so pay particular attention to your facial grooming, the appearance of your teeth, the neatness of your hair, and your choice of upper body clothes. In addition to paying special attention to the part of you that will be seen, you also want to recognize how video transmission affects colors and patterns. Choose dark clothing and avoid red clothing. In addition, avoid patterns. Imagine how that pattern will look when broken up by the transmission. If you want to see the effect of patterns for yourself, watch people's clothing on television. See how patterns sometimes look as if they have lives of their own. The effect is even more exaggerated in Internet transmissions. Again, because of the technical peculiarities of the systems, light blue is a better choice for a shirt or blouse color than white. White does not transmit well.

Practice speaking while sitting up straight and leaning slightly forward. This gives you a position similar to the one you would naturally assume in the interview situation. Avoid fidgeting. Remember that when you jiggle your feet or legs it affects your upper body. A lot of hand movements can also be distracting. Of course, no one expects you to sit perfectly still either. You might actually try to practice speaking in front of a mirror while sitting in a chair. As you speak during the practice, notice how your head and shoulders look and make corrections that you think will improve your appearance.

There is no magic Internet bullet for bringing about relaxation. And there is no reason why Internet interviewing, in and of itself, should be more or less tension-provoking. So how can technology help you prepare emotionally for the interview? If you can possibly get access to the equipment that you will be using in the video-conferencing interview, practice using it. Even if you can't actually use it, go to the center where the equipment is located and learn what you can about how it works and what you will be expected to do. We almost always feel safer, less nervous, when we know what to expect rather than when we imagine dozens of possible scenarios, none of which may be correct.

Just as you used the Internet to find information about jobs, you can use it to find information about meditation and visualization. I do not suggest using Internet counselors or therapists because there is no control over who is offering the services, how they have been educated and trained, or even who they really are. But you can find objective information about relaxation techniques on the Internet just as you can find it in books in the library.

Do not forget the technologies of compact disc and audiocassette players. You can use compact discs or audio-tapes of music that relaxes you to help you work against any tension. Some people prefer particular classical music selections. Others will find what they want in the New Age section of their music stores. Hal Lingerman's book, *The Healing Energies of Music,* provides lists of compact discs that can calm you down or raise your spirits as needed. I have produced the audiotape series *Head and Heart to Career Success* that helps the listener use relaxation and visualization to improve resumes and reach interview success.

The key advice to answering the question is: Listen! This becomes even more important when participating in Internet interviewing. The biggest flaw in the systems is a time lag. This means that you hear the words of the interviewer several seconds after they are spoken. As you watch the interviewer's lips you will see the words being formed, but they will not reach your ears as immediately as they do in face-to-face conversations. Both Marty Jones of Hewlett-Packard and Julie Dines of Bankers Trust, experienced executives in the forefront of Internet interviewing, stressed the importance of listening, of waiting to be sure the interviewer has really finished the question before you respond. You do not want to "step on someone else's lines" especially when you want to show how responsive you are in interpersonal situations.

Good equipment means you do not need to shout. Speak in a normal tone of voice. Address your answers to the interviewer.

Do not bring a friend to the interview. Because the interviewer is not in the room your friend may feel he or she can whisper to you or otherwise help you. This behavior will not only distract you, but your friend's remarks will probably be heard by the interviewer. Remember, although the interviewer is not in the same room, he or she can probably hear just about everything in the room—just as in a face-to-face interview.

Remember to sit forward rather than slouching in your chair. Remember to avoid fidgeting. Look at the interviewer just as you would in a face-to-face interview. Avoid focusing on your own image. Before you leave for the interview, be sure to look over your lists of strengths so you are ready to answer all questions.

Summary Worksheet

This chapter took you through seven steps to a winning interview. Look over the checklist below to be sure you have worked on all parts of the seven steps.

———— I have sheets prepared to make appointments for interviews, and I know what information I need.

———— I have thought about my strengths and my weaknesses.

———— I understand the requirements of the job or jobs I am looking for.

———— I know how my skills and knowledge meet the job requirements.

———— I know how to discuss my weaknesses or limitations.

———— I know how I want to look on the day of a job interview.

———— I have cleaned and prepared the clothes I will wear.

———— I know how to use my nervous energy.

———— I know the kinds of questions to expect and some ways to answer them.

———— I am prepared to listen before I answer.

KEEPING YOUR JOB

Part II

Hired!—Finding Out the Facts 5

You've done it! You've received a job offer. Now you want to be sure that you will be successful on your first job. One of the keys to success is knowing that you are in the right job. The first part of this chapter is about questions you will be sure you want answered *before* you accept the job.

Once you are on the job, there is more basic information that you need: information about your responsibilities and your rewards and how the company or organization works, and information about key people. This chapter is designed to help you find and organize that information so that you can fit in easily to your new job.

Should I Accept This Job?

During the interview, the employer had the opportunity to ask you questions about yourself. In a sense, at that point you were the seller, selling your services, and the employer was the buyer, deciding whether you have the services the company needs. Once the employer offers you a job, the focus changes. Now it is up to you to be sure that you want to accept the job.

In order to make the decision about whether or not you want a particular job, you have to think ahead of time about what you expect from a job. You have already made a choice about the type of work you will do by the kinds of jobs for which you are applying. However, there are often differences in what different companies or organizations offer to their employees, as well as differences in what they expect from them. Seven important ways in which particular jobs or companies can differ follow. As you look at this list, you will see that there is no such thing as a good or bad company. What appeals to one worker may not be desirable to another. Think about what appeals to you.

Seven areas to consider before accepting a job

1. *Work schedule.* Are the hours regular or irregular? Is evening or weekend work expected? Is there overtime?

2. *Work setting.* Is most of the work indoors in an office, store, factory, or shop? Is most of the work outdoors? Is it a combination of the two?

3. *Travel.* Does this job require local travel, travel within the city or nearby areas? Does this job require out-of-town travel?

4. *Salary.* What salary is being paid for this job? Is the salary determined on an annual, monthly, weekly, or hourly basis?

5. *Benefits.* What additional benefits are offered? Is health insurance paid for by the company? Is there reimbursement for additional education?

6. *Advancement.* Are there possibilities for moving up within this organization or will I have to move out to move up?

7. *Permanence.* Is this job temporary or "permanent"? (There is no such thing as a *truly* permanent job, but some jobs start out as temporary. They often provide a good way to get beginning experience.) Am I on the staff, working on a contract, or is the work seasonal with layoffs during slow periods?

Once you have decided upon the areas that are important to you, you are ready to ask questions after you have been offered the job.

Remember, until you have been offered that job, you are the seller. Before you talk about price, you want to convince the employer that you are the best possible person for the job. Many employers when interviewed said that the worst thing a person could do was to sound as if he or she just wanted the most money for the least amount of work. Of course, you do want the best possible salary for the work you do, but the important thing in the interview is to communicate how important the actual work is to you. Sometimes during the interview, you will be asked if you have any questions. A good question to ask is: "What will be the major responsibilities of this job?"

On the next page, you will find a Job Offer Worksheet. It lists many questions you can ask an employer once you have been offered the job. Look over the Job Offer Worksheet. Put a check next to each question that is important to you. Then fill in your ideal (but realistic) answer, the answer that would make you say, "Yes, this job is for me." When you have been offered a job, ask the questions that are important to you. Finally, compare the employer's answers with your ideal answers. You have to remember that no job is perfect. What you will be looking for in an actual job offer is the best possible combination of your ideals and the company's reality.

You may want to make copies of this worksheet so that you can use it for more than one offer.

Job Offer Worksheet

_____ 1. What is my starting salary?

Your Desire _____

Actual Offer _____

_____ 2. What are the hours and days of work?

Your Desire _____

Actual Offer _____

_____ 3. Is there overtime work?

Your Desire _____

Actual Offer _____

_____ 4. How will I be paid for overtime? extra pay? time off?

Your Desire

Actual Offer _____

_____ 5. How are salary increases determined?

Your Desire _____

Actual Offer _____

_____ 6. What kind of health insurance plan will I get?

Your Desire _____

Actual Offer _____

_____ 7. Who pays for the health insurance?

Your Desire _____

Actual Offer _____

_____ 8. Is there any reimbursement for college, graduate school, or other training?

Your Desire _____

Actual Offer _____

_____ 9. Is there any local or out-of-town travel?

Your Desire _____

Actual Offer _____

—————10. How will I be reimbursed for work-related travel expenses?

      Your Desire _____

      Actual Offer _____

—————11. How many vacation days do I get a year?

      Your Desire _____

      Actual Offer _____

—————12. What restrictions are there, if any, on taking vacations?

      Your Desire _____

      Actual Offer _____

—————13. What is the organization's sick leave policy?

      Your Desire _____

      Actual Offer _____

—————14. Is there a union I must join?

      Your Desire _____

      Actual Offer _____

The First Days— Fitting in Easily

Some large companies provide an orientation to all new employees on one of the first days they work. The purpose of an orientation is to get you started with all the facts you need about the company and your job. Orienting someone means pointing that person in the right direction. Whether or not your company does this, there is essential information you will want to get so you can move in the right direction. This information will make you more comfortable on the job and make you a more valuable employee. It will also help you begin to get ahead as soon as you get there.

Your first job may be in a factory, an office, a store, a hospital, or any one of dozens of other settings. Some of the information you need will vary with the kind of job you have, but some of it is basic. Sometimes all you need to know can seem overwhelming, but if it is broken down into smaller parts, you can see that some of the information you will find out very easily just in the course of events. You may want to ask your immediate supervisor for some of the information. Other information you will get from your coworkers. Some information will come to you through your own observations.

In the pages that follow, there are ten worksheets that deal with different times and aspects of the workday. They begin with your arrival and end with your leaving at the close of a workday. In between, they deal with such things as key people, getting supplies, and taking lunch. Look all of them over. Select the ones that have meaning for you in the job you have accepted or expect to take. Once on the job, find out the answers to the questions that apply to you.

Orientation Worksheet 1—Arrival

The information on this worksheet will help you get off to a good start every day.

1. What time am I expected at work?

_____

2. How does anyone know I am there? Do I punch a time clock?

_____

3. At what time is the office or shop unlocked?

_____

_____

_____

_____

4. What do I do if I get there and it's locked?

_____

_____

5. Where do I get the tools or supplies I need to start work each day?

_____

_____

_____

_____

_____

_____

6. Exactly where do I report?

_____

_____

_____

_____

_____

_____

_____

Orientation Worksheet 2—Key People

It is very important that you learn the names of people as quickly as possible. If you are in an office, one of the good ways to do this is to keep an index card on your desk and just jot down the names of people as you meet them, with some way for you to remember who they are. Eventually you will not need that help. You will know all the people who will be important in your work life.

1. What is the name of my immediate supervisor?

_____

_____

_____

2. How do I see that person? Is he or she right there? Do I telephone? Do I need an appointment?

_____

_____

3. What is the name of the president of the company? the head of the division in which I am working?

_____

_____

_____

4. What are the names of the coworkers who are working closest to me?

_____

_____

_____

_____

5. Who are the other people I have identified as important in the organization or in my work?

_____

_____

_____

_____

_____

Orientation Worksheet 3—Responsibilities

This worksheet is important to every worker, new and experienced. There is no job without responsibilities.

1. What tasks am I supposed to do?

_____

_____

_____

_____

_____

_____

_____

2. Am I supposed to get started by myself or wait for instructions?

_____

_____

_____

_____

_____

_____

_____

3. Who gives me instructions?

_____

_____

_____

_____

4. What do I do when I have finished the work I was asked to do?

_____

_____

_____

_____

_____

_____

Orientation Worksheet 4—Tools, Equipment, and Supplies

This worksheet is particularly important if you are working in a job where you need to use a lot of objects.

1. What are the major tools or supplies I need?

_____

_____

_____

_____

_____

2. Who is responsible for supplying them?

_____

_____

_____

3. Where do I get supplies? Is there any procedure for requesting them or signing them out?

_____

_____

_____

4. What do I do if a piece of equipment is not working?

_____

_____

_____

5. If I am asked to lay out money to buy something for the office or shop, or to go somewhere, how do I get it back?

_____

_____

_____

_____

Orientation Worksheet 5—Dealing with the Public

In some jobs, most of the work involves dealing with the public, that is, with people outside the company. Often these are the customers or clients of the company. Most of these questions are for people working in sales.

1. To what extent am I supposed to deal with customers or clients?

_____

_____

_____

_____

_____

2. How do I handle cash payments from customers?

_____

_____

_____

_____

3. How do I handle charge payments from customers?

_____

_____

_____

_____

4. What is the company policy on complaints?

_____

_____

_____

_____

_____

Orientation Worksheet 6—Lunch and Other Breaks

Use this worksheet to help you figure out company policy on lunch and other breaks, as well as things you can do during those periods to relax and enjoy your time.

1. How much time is allowed for lunch?

_____

2. Is there some particular schedule I must follow when I take lunch?

_____

3. Is there a company cafeteria where I can buy food or a company lunchroom where I can bring food and eat in?

_____

4. What are some of the good and inexpensive eating places nearby?

_____

_____

_____

_____

5. If I bring lunch from home, is there a refrigerator I can use?

_____

6. Are there some interesting places to walk during lunch?

_____

_____

_____

_____

7. Are there any other scheduled breaks?

_____

_____

_____

_____

8. Where are the restrooms? Do I need a key?

_____

Orientation Worksheet 7—Getting Paid

This worksheet will help you understand your paycheck and be sure that it is correct. You should know your salary when you are hired. However, your gross salary is not the same as your net salary. Your gross salary is the amount the employer is paying for your work. Then deductions are made for federal, state, and sometimes local taxes and for social security. There may be other deductions for health insurance and union dues. On some of these you may have a choice. What is left after deductions is your net pay.

1. When am I paid?

_____

2. What will my gross salary each pay period be?

_____

3. Am I being paid on a hourly basis, in which the pay will be different each pay period based on the number of hours I worked, or am I being paid the same amount each pay period?

_____

_____

_____

4. If I am being paid on an hourly basis, how is my pay figured?

_____

_____

_____

_____

5. What deductions, besides tax and social security, will there be and how much will each one be?

_____

_____

_____

6. If I am entitled to overtime pay, when will I receive it?

_____

_____

Orientation Worksheet 8—Unions

Some jobs and some companies are unionized; that is, a union has won the right to carry out collective bargaining on behalf of the workers—that's you.

There are four types of memberships. Where there is an *open shop*, you will find union and nonunion workers employed side by side. You are free to join or not to join. Where there is an *agency shop*, you will also fine union and nonunion people working together. However, everyone must pay an agency fee to the union. You may decide to join or not to join. If you join, you will pay somewhat more than the agency fee, and you will get additional benefits. Where there is a *union shop*, all employees must become union members once they get the job. You will have no choice about joining. Where there is a *closed shop*, you must be a member of the union before you get the job. If you have gotten the job, you are already a member.

1. Is there a union?

_____

2. What type of shop is it?

_____

3. What are the benefits of union membership?

_____

_____

_____

4. What is the cost of union membership?

_____

5. Who is my union representative?

_____

Orientation Worksheet 9—Getting Sick and Staying Well

No one plans to get sick, but unfortunately most of us do find ourselves with a cold or the flu from time to time. While employers expect you to be on the job regularly, no one wants you to come to work if you are too sick to perform your job. It is important that you call as soon as you know you are not going to be able to come to work. You should make the call yourself, unless you are really too sick to do so. Having someone else call for you does not convince your employer that you are sick, and it does not give the employer the chance to ask you any questions about the work you have been doing.

1. What is the company policy on sick leave?

_____

_____

2. If I am sick, whom should I call?

_____

3. What is that person's or office's telephone number and extension?

_____

4. When I return, is there any special procedure to follow?

_____

_____

_____

5. How do I report sick days on the time clock or time report sheets?

_____

_____

_____

_____

_____

6. Does my company offer any health maintenance of fitness services?

_____

_____

_____

_____

_____

_____

Orientation Worksheet 10—End of the Day

Just as you want to arrive on time and make a good first impression, it is important to learn not only the company rules but the customs for the end of the day.

1. At what time do I officially finish work?

_____

_____

_____

2. If I am in the middle of a job, what am I expected to do?

_____

_____

_____

3. Am I supposed to wait for someone to take over my work, to relieve me?

_____

_____

_____

4. Whose job it is to turn off any equipment at the end of the day?

_____

_____

_____

5. Whose job is it to lock away valuable items?

_____

_____

_____

6. Is there a safe place to leave my tools?

_____

_____

_____

7. Whose job is it to close the office or lock the shop at the end of the day?

_____

_____

_____

Summary Worksheet

In this chapter you figured out the information you will want to have before you accept a job and the information you need once you are on the job. Probably there was information suggested in the chapter that did not interest you or that did not have anything to do with your work. You also learned how to sort out the information that is important to you from all the kinds of information listed. Use the checklist below to confirm your thinking.

_____ I know what is important to me in looking for a job.

_____ I know not to introduce questions of salary and hours until after I have been offered a job.

_____ I have thought about what it means to orient myself to a job, to point myself in the right direction.

_____ I have looked over all the orientation worksheets and picked out the questions that have meaning for me.

_____ I know how to begin the day.

_____ I know how to deal with customers or clients.

_____ I know the names of the people who are important to me in the organization.

_____ I know how to find or store tools and supplies.

_____ I know about lunch and other breaks.

_____ I know what to do if I will be sick and unable to work.

_____ I know how to end the day.

On-the-Job Success

6

Now that you are on the job and have mastered the basics that you need to know, you want to be sure that you know what behaviors will bring success. Whether you want to keep this job, get promoted within the organization, or find a different job somewhere else, a key to your future success is your present success.

In the first part of this book, you took a look at the habits and skills of success and saw how those applied to getting a job. Now you can examine what it takes to be successful once the job is yours. A large part of being successful rests in recognizing our interdependence with other people. Interdependence does not mean that we depend or lean on others for help. It also doesn't mean that it's our job to give help to others. Interdependence is bigger than either of these ideas. It means we cannot function at all without each other.

Necessary Skills for On-the-Job Success

The United States Department of Labor has been studying the nature of on-the-job success. It has reported its findings and conclusions in a booklet, *What Work Requires of School: A SCANS Report for America 2000.* The word *SCANS* in the title stands for the Secretary's Commission on Achieving Necessary Skills. It is the *necessary skills* part that is of greatest interest to us. Whether you learn these skills in school or on your own, they are the skills that employers want in their employees—that's you—in order to have successful, competitive businesses. Just as a business can get ahead by having employees with these skills, you can be successful by being an employee who has them.

Before we get to the skills themselves, we need to understand two more things. First, these skills are different from the technical knowledge that you may need on the job. Of course, a word-processing machine operator must know how to type and use software, and a salesperson must know the product, the prices, and how to persuade people to buy. But they both need particular personal and interpersonal competencies to use their knowledge in effective ways. The second important idea is that the skills were identified nationwide as being important. So you can be sure that they are important to employers in your community, whether you live in a large city, a suburb, or a farming area.

The necessary skills are built on a three-part foundation. The first part of the foundation is the *basic skills.* The basis skills include reading, writing, arithmetic, listening, and speaking. The second part is *thinking skills.* Thinking skills include decision making, problem solving, reasoning, and knowing how to learn. But the area of skills most related to this section of the book is the area of *personal skills.* There are five personal skills listed in the SCANS Report. They are as follows:

1. Responsibility—You work hard toward reaching a goal.

2. Self-esteem—You believe in your own self-worth.

3. Sociability—You show understanding of others and act with politeness in group settings.

4. Self-management—You set your own goals, measure your own progress, and show self-control.

5. Integrity/Honesty—You choose the ethical course of action.

In addition to the basic skills, the report identifies competencies—things every worker should be able to do. Eight of these competencies are very important to you as a beginning worker. It will not surprise you by now to learn that one of the main areas of competency is in the "interpersonal" area. Here are the eight competencies. Mastering the first four will bring you a long way toward satisfying the overall goal of working well with others.

1. You work well as a member of a team and you contribute to the group effort.

2. You know how to serve clients or customers.

3. You are willing to negotiate to help resolve differences of opinion or of interests.

4. You work well with men and women from diverse backgrounds.

5. You know how to allocate your time and follow schedules to meet the goals of your work.

6. You know how to acquire, store, and use materials efficiently.

7. You can acquire, evaluate, and maintain up-to-date information.

8. You know how to choose appropriate procedures, tools, or equipment.

Of course, you are not expected to memorize these lists. The important thing is not that there are five of one kind of skill and eight of another. The important thing is for each of use to learn how to get the best from ourselves and how to work well with others. The suggestions and the worksheets in the previous chapter helped you gather information you need to get off to a good start on the job. This chapter gives you food for thought on working with others, including bosses, customers, coworkers, and people who may report to you.

A checklist of skills   Take a look at the checklist that follows. It is similar to the one you completed at the end of the first chapter. These items are also drawn from "The National Career Development Guidelines" of the National Occupational Information Coordinating Committee. Use it as you did the first one, to identify your current strengths and to double-check when you complete this section of the book, to see what you have learned.

Ready to Keep a Job
A Checklist of Indicators

Directions: In the first column, place a check next to those job-seeking skills you think you have "Now." Place a question mark next to the ones you would like to find out more about. If you are uncertain, leave the space blank. As you read through this book, come back and place a plus sign in the second column, "Later," when you think you have really mastered a particular skill.

Now	*Later*	*Essential Skills for Job Seeking*
———	———	1. Demonstrate interpersonal skills required for working with, and for, others.
———	———	2. Describe appropriate employer and employee interactions in various situations.
———	———	3. Demonstrate how to express feelings, reactions, and ideas in an appropriate manner.
———	———	4. Describe healthy ways of dealing with stress.
———	———	5. Demonstrate positive work attitudes and behaviors.
———	———	6. Demonstrate a realistic understanding of self.

———   ———   7. Demonstrate behaviors, attitudes, and skills that work to eliminate stereotyping in education, family, and work environments.

———   ———   8. Describe how family and leisure functions affect occupational roles and decisions.

———   ———   9. Demonstrate confidence in the ability to learn new things.

———   ———   10. Describe community and organizational resources that support education and training.

What Employers Want

Some people find it hard to understand what an employer is looking for and why he or she prefers one employee over another. They think the employer is just playing favorites or that the employee is just bending over backwards to be liked, trying to be the "teacher's pet." Well, work is not like school. In school, teachers do have to try to be fair to everyone. At work, employers try to identify the best employees because better workers mean a more successful business operation. The best workers get the rewards of promotions and raises.

Research with employers and with recently hired employees reveals what employers are looking for and what most workers need to learn if they are to be successful. This chapter will let you in on the findings of the research and present you with situations or case studies to help you see things from both the worker's and the employer's points of view.

In general, research about what makes a worker successful, what can make you successful on the job, focuses on attitude. Before you are hired, the boss can find out if you really know how to type or if you have learned how to replace brakes. He or she cannot know how you will behave with other people while you are doing it. Your boss cannot know whether you will work hard or look for the easiest way out. He or she cannot know whether you will come to work late and be absent frequently, or whether you can be depended upon to be there.

There are ten skills for success that we will focus on in this chapter. These skills were drawn from several studies conducted with employers in a wide range of industries in different parts of the United States, as well as from the SCANS Report mentioned in the last chapter. Knowing something about these studies may help you see how similar employers are in their desires for the ideal or best possible employee.

"Termination is usually the result of poor use of time, poor attendance, and poor attitude rather than the result of incompetence." This was one of the key findings of a study conducted among employers of two vocational training institutions' graduates in Wisconsin. The same study found that, "demonstrating a willingness to learn, being punctual and regular in attendance, and keeping supervisors informed are important for the new worker."

Lack of responsibility, lack of initiative, and absenteeism were the three most troublesome problems with beginning workers, according to employers of beginning office workers. This study was conducted in the state of

New York and included businesses in both New York City and the rural areas of the state.

Efficiency, courtesy, pride, and enthusiasm in one's work were found to be the most important worker qualities in a study of more than two hundred businesses in New Hampshire.

"Employers find that most job applicants are not lacking as much in knowing how to do the job, the technical skills, as they are in attitude toward work and the ability to communicate with and relate to others." This was the finding of a three-year study that included employers of office workers; computer specialists; freight and traffic handlers; salespeople; workers in international trade; social service workers; people in audio-visual, printing, and energy industry occupations; and many others.

In another study in New York City, employers of recent high school graduates were asked to rank fourteen worker traits that had already been identified as important on-the-job qualities. The employers ranked the following three traits highest:

1. Follows through on a job assignment

2. Is a productive worker

3. Comes to work regularly

If you look over the ten Orientation Worksheets in Chapter 5, you will see how you are already beginning to identify and exhibit some of the skills for success identified in the studies. Getting information is part of adapting to an organization. Certainly you cannot get to work on time if you don't know what time you are expected, and you cannot let your supervisor know what you are doing if you don't know who your supervisor is. Now it is time to zero in on the ten skills for success. Each of the skills is discussed in the pages that follow, with examples from both the employer's and employee's points of view.

Ten skills for success

1. Be dependable—give a full day's work.

2. Work well with your supervisor.

3. Know when to ask questions.

4. Cooperate with coworkers.

5. Carry out your responsibilities.

6. Take pride in what you do.

7. Show initiative—learn new skills, take on new tasks.

8. Look your best.

9. Control your emotions.

10. Become a part of the organization.

Be Dependable— Give a Full Day's Work

How boring. It seems as if all of your life people have been telling you to be on time. Teachers were always saying terrible things would happen if you were late to school. But when you were late, what happened? You got a late pass. Well, maybe your grades would have been better if you had gotten there. That all seems unimportant now.

A job is different. You really need to get there on time because the company or organization is waiting for you to perform your work. Unlike school, where each person's work is separate from every other person's, wherever you are working there is a chain of work in which one person's successful performance depends upon another's.

Imagine you are a word processor in an office. Your supervisor, Mr. McNeill, has to give a report to the president of the company, Ms. Chase. Mr. McNeill spent most of last night writing the report. He is waiting for you to type it. Ms. Chase is waiting to receive it. Imagine how Mr. McNeill feels when you walk in a few minutes early ready to work. Imagine how he feels if you get there half an hour late.

Now picture yourself as a general worker in a local hardware and locksmith shop. Your boss, Mr. Folger, opens the shop at 7:30 in the morning. He immediately gets a call from Ms. Elson who says that he must come to help her fix the broken lock on her front door. She cannot leave. She cannot take her children to school or get to work herself because the door will be wide open. Mr. Folger assures Ms. Elson that he will be there at 8:15, since he knows you get in at 8:00 and can take over in the shop. Imagine how Mr. Folger feels when he sees you walk in at 7:45. Imagine how he feels when you walk in at 8:20.

You need to be on time so that you are a strong link in the chain of work. You want to be on time for another reason. Many of the skills for success that we will be discussing in this chapter are hard to assess. It is very easy, on the other hand, to see if someone is there or not there. Often supervisors and employers are willing to give a new worker a chance to work out. They don't jump on every little mistake. They are patient. However, if they get to the point where they are about to give up on you, your not being where you are supposed to be is often the final straw.

Being dependable means not only getting to work on time but being on the job. That means taking no more time for lunch than you are entitled to and not goofing off. Some people get to work all right. Then they spend a lot of time, more than they need, in the restroom or visiting with coworkers. Other people never seem to get back from some errand outside the office as quickly as most people do. All of these undependable behaviors mean that your employer is not getting a full day's work for the money being paid you. No one wants to be cheated.

Situation Study 1

Alice Edwards had found the job she wanted. She was going to work as an administrative assistant in an insurance company, and she had the chance to attend classes to learn the latest in database programs.

The first day was fine. She was expected at work at 9:00 A.M. She was happy to see that she got to the building just on time. She had a little trouble finding the right office, but she was there before 9:30, and her new boss, Audrey Russell, was very sympathetic about her getting lost in the building.

After two months, Alice felt she was doing very well on the job. She had improved her word processing skills and was scheduled for the database management class in just a few weeks. She had missed the first training session because she had to leave early every day for a week to go to the dentist. Ms. Russell had said she could do it but hadn't looked very happy about it. But what could Alice do? She had to go to the dentist.

Alice was quite surprised to be called into her boss's office that morning. It was 9:30, and Ms. Russell was waiting for her at her desk when she arrived. Ms. Russell said that Alice kept coming late and had missed time for the dentist and that this had to be improved or Alice would be fired! Alice explained that the bus she took left her off on the corner just at 9:00, and that meant she was just a little late each day. The next earlier bus would mean that Alice would have to leave her house forty-five minutes earlier. Audrey Russell seemed not to care and repeated that Alice would be fired if she kept missing work.

Imagine you are Alice Edwards.

How do you feel?

_____

_____

_____

_____

_____

_____

_____

What will you do?

_____

_____

_____

_____

_____

_____

_____

Imagine you are Audrey Russell.

How do you feel?

_____

_____

_____

_____

_____

_____

_____

_____

_____

_____

_____

_____

What will you do?

_____

_____

_____

_____

_____

_____

_____

_____

_____

_____

_____

(*Hint:* **Better late than never may soon become never.**)

Work Well with Your Supervisor

Once you accept a job, your supervisor or boss becomes a key person in your life. You may be one of many people that person supervises, or you may be her or his entire staff. Some people are very good at being supervisors. They know how to help the people working for them so that they bring out the best in all workers. Some supervisors are patient and fair with everyone. It is a good idea to expect behavior like that from your supervisor. However, sometimes you will not be so lucky, and your supervisor will be more difficult to get along with. It is your job to adapt to your supervisor.

One of the skills you can use to get along with your boss is the skill of listening. This skill was discussed at the end of Chapter 4 on interviewing. Remember to look at the person who is speaking to you and to pay attention to what that person is saying. Your boss will be giving you directions on what is expected of you and how to carry out your responsibilities. You cannot carry them out well if you have not heard them.

It is not a good idea to argue with your boss frequently, at least not when you are new on the job. You may think of ways you would prefer doing things over the ways that are explained. Maybe you learned some different techniques in school or on a part-time job. When you are new on a job, do things the way you are asked to do them. There is probably a reason that they are being done in a particular way. Sometimes the reason is not apparent. It may be because that is how the company has always done it. It may be that it is being done that way because it protects someone else who cannot do a particular task well. It may even be because it is the best way to do it. In the beginning, assume that the way you are being told is the right way. Then watch for a while and see if what you think is a better way would be an improvement. If you still think so, suggest it.

One newly employed worker, Jeff, was having a lot of trouble getting along with his boss, Mr. Sharp. Finally, Jeff figured out one of the problems. He realized that in school, teachers always had to listen to his ideas. That was their job—to help him figure out ideas and then to listen to them. While Mr. Sharp did have to teach him what to do, he did not have to listen to his ideas, nor did he want to.

Part of getting along with your supervisor is being able to accept constructive criticism. From your boss's point of view, all criticism is constructive. You are being criticized to improve your performance so that its contribution to the product or service of your organization will be better.

Again, listening is the first step. Following through and making changes in how you do things is the second step. This does not mean that you should never question anything or make any suggestions. It does mean that it takes some time to get to know how and why things are done in an organization, and you need to be accepting for a while before presenting your opinion.

If you find you disagree with your supervisor, it is never a good idea to express this disagreement while you are being criticized. It is better to listen, think about the criticism, and then if you disagree with part of it say something like, "I have been thinking about your suggestion that I do A before B and then do C. It seems to me that I might save time if I did A first, then B and C together. What do you think?"

Loyalty to the organization is considered very important by most employers. You might wonder, especially if you are working in a large corporation, how you can show you are loyal to some product or service that is far removed from you. One of the ways is by being loyal to your supervisor. It is not a good idea to spend a lot of time criticizing your supervisor even when other people are griping. It is an even worse idea to do this with people in other divisions or units of the same organization. Work places are often big rumor mills. Until you make some friends you know you can trust, the best way to air your feelings about people at work is to talk to people who don't know them—people at home.

Going to your boss's supervisor to complain about something or someone, particularly about your boss, rarely works to your advantage. Sometimes when you are hired, you know someone higher up in the organization than your immediate supervisor. You will have to work extra hard in that case to convince your supervisor that you are loyal. If you go over your boss's head, her or his supervisor may very well interpret that as disloyalty and act to protect your boss, not you.

Go over your boss's head only if what you are trying to accomplish is very important to you; you have explored every other way to accomplish your goal; and you are willing to lose a great deal, perhaps even your job.

Situation Study 2

Frank Green was hired by a large corporation to work in the customer relations division. One of his tasks was dealing with customers when they had complaints. Another was setting up training sessions for salespeople.

Evelyn Harrod, Frank's supervisor, at first thought that Frank was going to work out very well. He was very patient with customers and was able to handle their complaints well. Ms. Harrod had only one complaint. Sometimes Mr. Green went so out of his way to help customers that he could not get enough of his other work done. She explained this to him, but he said, "Don't you want me to satisfy the customers?" She tried to explain about limiting his time with each customer. Frank said, "I just have to take the amount of time it takes to make each one really feel good.

When the time for the first training meeting came, Ms. Harrod asked Mr. Green to prepare a package of materials for each salesperson.

When the day of the training arrived, Ms. Harrod saw that instead of preparing one package of twelve items for each person, there were twelve stacks of papers and each person would have to be asked to take one. She felt this would take unnecessary time and she could not be sure each person had all of the materials. In addition, it seemed to indicate a poorly planned meeting, one that would not get off to a good, crisp start.

At the end of the meeting, she spoke to Mr. Green about not following her instructions. He said, "I didn't think it mattered, and I didn't have time to do it your way. They got all the material, didn't they?"

Imagine you are Frank Green.

How do you feel?

_____

_____

_____

_____

_____

_____

_____

What will you do?

_____

_____

_____

_____

_____

_____

_____

Imagine you are Evelyn Harrod.

How do you feel?

_____

_____

_____

_____

_____

_____

_____

_____

_____

_____

_____

What will you do?

_____

_____

_____

_____

_____

_____

_____

_____

_____

_____

_____

(*Hint:* **Your time is my time.**)

Know When to Ask Questions

Part of getting along with your supervisor is knowing when and how to ask questions. Some supervisors like to structure everything and will welcome many questions from you. Others would prefer that you act more on your own. You will have to feel your way. However, there are two good basic rules:

1. If you really don't know how to do something, ask.

2. If you know the answer, don't ask.

Some people ask questions as a way of challenging their bosses. Those are questions like, "Are you sure you want me to do it *that* way?" or "Wouldn't you like me to try to do this the other way?" Those are generally not effective ways of presenting an opinion. If you want to suggest a change, wait until you are sure of yourself, then make the suggestion clearly. "I see another way to do that. I would like to describe it to you. When would be a good time?"

In general, when you are a new worker, it is better to ask questions about how to do something than not to ask. When you ask a question, be ready for the answer. Listen to the answer so you won't have to ask the same question again. Ask the question with a paper and pencil handy so that you can jot down the details of the answer.

Cooperate with Coworkers

Just as you need to get along with your boss, you need to find ways of working with your coworkers, the people around you. This is important for several reasons. First of all, it is important to you. Getting along with the people around you will make your day easier and more pleasant. Experienced workers around you can often show you the ropes and help you figure out how things get done in your organization.

Getting along with your coworkers is also important to the company. In talking about the first success skill, dependability, we talked about the chain of work. In addition, there is a concept called team effort. Many jobs require several people working alongside each other for completion. If you are working on an assembly line, you can picture how each person's completion of a job leads to the next person's work. Now picture a situation like working in a hospital. The doctors, nurses, aides, and technicians of various kinds all work to help one patient. Both a chain of work and teamwork are needed.

In addition to the need for teamwork, better work is done when people feel good about their relationships with each other. If people feel they have no friends, that everyone around them is hostile and an enemy, then too much time is spent watching one's back rather than working.

This does not mean you have to accept everyone as your great buddy from the first day you are at work. In most places, someone will ask you to have lunch or will walk with you as you leave. Be open to friendly gestures. Listen to people. Choose friends at work as you would choose them elsewhere. However, don't divide your coworkers into mental lists of friends and enemies. Most will not be either. They will simply be your coworkers.

There are two kinds of behavior that really turn people off at work. One is not doing your share of the work. The other is being a know-it-all. You can avoid the first by doing your work. You can avoid the second by staying out of other people's work and by not talking about all you know, especially about things that are not your job.

Situation Study 3

Barbara Masters had been hired to do the billing for a large mail order company. Jerry Noff, her boss, had explained that things were really in a mess because the previous bookkeeper had not known what he was doing. Barbara felt she could do the work and was glad to get a first job that had a challenge to it.

When Barbara got the records that had to be corrected and had to result in actual bills, she saw that it was even worse than Mr. Noff had said. She looked things over and saw a way to do it that she thought was better. Barbara explained her method to Mr. Noff, and he said, "Ms. Masters, I would appreciate anything you can do to straighten this out as quickly as possible. It sounds like you know what you're talking about. Go right ahead."

Barbara got to work, and her method was working. But the work was tedious and time-consuming. She had to look at all these poorly written records. She decided she had to take a break, so she walked away from her desk for a few minutes to talk to Mary Harris, whom she'd met at lunch.

Mary was working on a microcomputer. Barbara knew a lot about computers. She had taken computer courses and liked to fool around with programming. Barbara watched Mary for a few minutes. She was working on a new record system that would include billing. Barbara realized that Mary was using the ABC software, when it was obvious that XYZ would be much better. "Wait a minute," Barbara said to Mary. "Why don't you switch to XYZ? You could write that program much more easily, and it could hold a lot more data."

Imagine you are Mary Harris.

How do you feel?

_____

_____

_____

_____

_____

_____

_____

What will you do?

_____

_____

_____

_____

_____

_____

_____

_____

Imagine you are Barbara Masters.

How do you feel?

_____

_____

_____

_____

_____

_____

_____

What will you do?

_____

_____

_____

_____

_____

_____

_____

Imagine you are Jerry Noff.

How do you feel?

_____

_____

_____

_____

_____

_____

What will you do?

_____

_____

_____

_____

_____

_____

_____

(*Hint:* Carry your own weight—not others'.)

Carry Out Your Responsibilities

Every job has its responsibilities. These include the tasks you are expected to carry out and the methods you are supposed to use to carry them out. Responsibilities also include knowing how to take proper care of the tools, equipment, or supplies you use and following the work schedule that has been laid out for you. A person who carries out all of his or her responsibilities as expected is a person who can be trusted with more responsibilities. That person is considered trustworthy by the supervisor.

In the previous chapter, you used orientation worksheets to help identify your responsibilities. In Orientation Worksheet 3, you looked at your responsibilities. In Orientation Worksheet 4, you thought about tools, equipment, and supplies. It would be a good idea to look at those worksheets again now.

Once you know your responsibilities, it is up to you to carry them out. If you are avoiding some of them because you don't know how to do them, or you are afraid of not doing them well, it is a good idea to speak to your supervisor and get some help. It is better for you to admit you don't know something than to have your supervisor find out that you simply have not been doing it. The effect of your not carrying out your responsibilities goes beyond the poor impression it gives of you. It affects the chain of work and the teamwork of the organization.

There are a number of ways to demonstrate your trustworthiness. If you handle money—take cash for sales, get reimbursed for expenses, buy materials for the company—you must always be sure that your dealings are completely honest and that your records of these dealings are up-to-date and correct. If your schedule is flexible and sometimes your work is in the office and sometimes outside, it is a good idea to make sure that your supervisor knows where you are at all times.

Situation Study 4

Robert Broom was hired as a truck driver for a food company. His job was to drive the truck in the mornings on a set route, making deliveries to particular customers. While he was on his route in the morning, calls came from other customers for special deliveries to be made in the afternoon. Some afternoons there were a lot of deliveries, on others very few.

Robert liked his job. It gave him a chance to be outside, and he enjoyed driving. He liked the few minutes he had to chat with each customer. After a few weeks, he saw that by varying the route just a little, he could serve all the customers and end up in a different place for lunch every day. He didn't like the afternoons as much. If there were too few special deliveries, he just sat around in the office with nothing to do but wait.

Steven Peters was Robert's boss and the owner of the company. He liked Robert and thought he did a good job. He kept the truck nice and clean and was always there on time in the morning.

One day Steven got a call from an afternoon customer that was urgent. Steven needed to get to Robert in the middle of the morning so that Robert could interrupt his deliveries and serve this customer. Steven got out the schedule of deliveries and figured out where Robert would be at that time of the morning. He called; Robert had been there half an hour earlier. He called a place further down the list; Robert had been there first thing in the morning.

Steven never caught up with Robert. The customer was unreasonable and said he would never deal with them again. When Robert got back to the office, Steven was very angry. He asked Robert where he had been. When Robert told him about the route changes, Steven said that Robert should stick to the route he had given him or quit.

Imagine you are Robert Broom.

How do you feel?

_____

_____

_____

What will you do?

_____

_____

_____

Imagine you are Steven Peters.

How do you feel?

_____

_____

_____

What will you do?

_____

_____

_____

Take Pride in What You Do

The sixth skill for success is often called conscientiousness. People who have this skill take pride in what they do. They see what they are doing as important work. They see their work through to the finish and consider it a finished piece of work even when it is part of a much larger operation.

There is no work that is not important. Some work is necessary for people's basic needs and others for their desires. All of it contributes to the country's economic health. It is true that some jobs get higher pay and some jobs have more prestige, but the pride in one's own work has nothing to do with that.

Employers look for workers who set high performance standards for themselves and whose work is of a high quality, even when doing so means that the employee had to put in some extra time or effort.

Some people will say, "It's not my job," or "Why should I care? They're earning the big bucks." One reason to care is because it feels better. Another reason for you to care is because extra effort is a key to success. Now that you have your first job, watch the people in your organization who are successful. You will see that many of them do things that others should be doing for them, things that are not their job. One of the big differences between people who just get by and people who succeed is the willingness to go the extra mile, to pitch in and help.

In an office, being conscientious may mean cleaning the plate of the photocopying machine and rerunning copies when you see that what you have done is all full of gray smudges. In a shop, being conscientious may mean going for a replacement tool or part when you see that the one you have will work, but not perfectly. In a store, being conscientious may mean being the one who replaces the shopping bags when the supply at your station has been used up.

Situation Study 5

Leonard Anderson and Carrie Curran were both somewhat new workers in the company. Carrie had been there six months, Leonard three. Carrie was a secretary. Leonard was a sales representative.

The company was planning to announce a new product. Everyone was very excited about it. Ellen Brock, who was Leonard and Carrie's supervisor and the head of the division responsible for the product, saw this as a big chance for the division, for everyone in it, and for herself.

Small replicas of the product had been made for everyone who would attend the announcement. This included the company bigwigs, the stockholders, and some major customers. Ellen had worked very hard on a one-page description of how to use the product. This was to be given out along with the replicas.

Ellen asked Leonard and Carrie to see that the product and a copy of the report were on each of the two hundred seats. A half hour before the meeting, Ellen went in to check the room. Half the seats had the product. Half had the reports. All the reports were poor copies.

Ellen was very upset. She called Leonard and Carrie into her office. Leonard said, "We ran out of replicas, and it's not my job to look for more." Carrie said, "I know where the replicas are, but he didn't ask me." "What about the copies?" asked Ellen. "Well," answered Carrie, "the photocopying machine is broken so I couldn't finish them." "She could have taken them down to the third floor. There's a machine there," muttered Leonard.

Imagine you are Carrie Curran.

How do you feel?

_____

_____

_____

_____

_____

_____

_____

What will you do?

_____

_____

_____

_____

_____

_____

_____

Imagine you are Leonard Anderson.

How do you feel?

_____

_____

_____

_____

_____

_____

What will you do?

_____

_____

_____

_____

_____

_____

Imagine you are Ellen Brock.

How do you feel?

_____

_____

_____

_____

_____

_____

What will you do?

_____

_____

_____

_____

_____

_____

Show Initiative—
Learn New Skills,
Take On New Tasks

Initiative is the big step beyond conscientiousness. Just as you want to do every job you are supposed to do to the best of your ability, you also want to look for opportunities to add responsibilities and learn new things.

In many organizations, promotion comes after you have earned it. This means that if you want to move up in a company, you often need to be willing to take on some new responsibilities before you are being paid to do so.

In earlier sections of this chapter, we stressed doing what you are told to do. That is good for the first few months on the job. After that, if you see a better way to do something that you think will be accepted, then you can suggest that to your boss. Some companies have suggestion boxes or formal ways of suggesting improvements.

Sometimes, you will have the opportunity to take on new responsibilities because some big job comes along and your organization is shorthanded. Sometimes the opportunity comes along because someone is away unexpectedly. Take these opportunities as soon as you feel you can carry them out well.

Some companies offer the opportunity to expand your knowledge through courses they offer or sponsor, or by paying your tuition. Sometimes courses are offered or sponsored by unions. Try to take advantage of those opportunities that interest you.

Look Your Best

When you are on the job, you will not only be dealing with the people around you, but you will also be representing your organization to the public. This means that you need to look your best *as appropriate to your job.* That last phrase is really the key.

Many suggestions about good grooming were given in Chapter 4 on interviewing. Once you get the job, it would be a good idea to look those over again. Clean teeth, hair, nails, and body are a first essential. Of course, you may be on a job where you get dirty during the course of the day. Whether that is the case or not, a daily bath or shower are essential parts of good hygiene. Let's face it—it is very difficult to work with someone who has bad breath or who has a body odor from an unwashed body or unlaundered clothes. This may seem less important as a success skill to you than the others, but it is one that many employers mentioned in the studies.

Your choice of clothes should be governed by the kind of work you do. Look around at how others in your company and industry dress, and try to dress similarly, exercising your own taste at the same time. In general, the more conservative industries, like banking and law, require more conservative dress. Some industries require that you wear uniforms. In still others, you have more freedom of choice.

In any case, be sure your clothes fit you well and are kept clean. Avoid wearing party clothes or very casual clothes like shorts to work unless you are in a business where such clothing is called for. Remember the key word is *appropriate.*

Control Your Emotions

While you are on the job, many stresses and frustrations can occur that will test your ability to control your emotions. It is difficult to say just how much expression one is allowed on the job because of the many different situations that can arise.

Of course, physical fighting is not only forbidden but can land you in jail with a charge of assault or battery. Hollering and screaming, no matter how angry you get, are also not desirable on-the-job behaviors, although you will see some people shout. Crying, except in the most trying circumstances, usually just embarrasses everyone around you.

It is important that you find ways to communicate with your supervisor and your coworkers that are effective and that do not escalate your emotions to the point of a loss of control. Talking things through before they get too bad works well in some circumstances. Sometimes, however, you have to wait until you or the other person cools off. Each situation must be judged on its own.

Since most jobs come with some stress, it is a good idea to have some ways of reducing its effect on you. Some people find that regular physical activity helps. They walk or jog regularly or belong to a gym or team. Some people practice meditation or relaxation techniques. Other people like to read, listen to music, or pursue a hobby. Now that you have your first full-time job, if you do not have some ways of decompressing and reducing your tensions, try to find them.

Situation Study 6

Remember Carrie and Leonard from the previous situation study? Things have not improved in that office.

Neither of them was fired as a result of the first situation. A few weeks later, Leonard had to complete his quarterly sales report, which had a lot of figures. He completed it and gave it to Carrie to type. When it was finished, he submitted it to Ellen, their boss.

When Ellen read it, it didn't make much sense. The sales, which should have totaled the same when added up by customer and added up by week, did not do so. She called Leonard in and asked him to look at the report and figure out what was wrong.

Leonard took the report back to his desk and took out the information he had in his files. Somehow in typing, two columns of numbers had gotten jumbled.

He went back to Ellen. "Well," he said, "this is all Carrie's fault. Look, she typed these two columns wrong."

Ellen said, "I'm glad it's not a big mistake, but I want you to know that I hold you responsible. Although Carrie typed it, it's your report and you have to be sure it's correct before you give it to me. Please correct it and have it retyped for tomorrow."

Ellen left the office for a meeting. On her way back, while still in the hall, she could hear a loud voice coming from the office. She walked in to see Leonard standing next to Carrie, who was at her desk.

He was shouting, "What is wrong with you? Are you an idiot? Or did you do this to me on purpose? You never liked me. I'm going to get even for this. Now, you type this and you'd better get it right!"

Imagine you are Leonard Anderson.

How do you feel?

_____

_____

_____

_____

_____

_____

What will you do?

_____

_____

_____

_____

_____

_____

Imagine you are Carrie Curran.

How do you feel?

_____

_____

_____

_____

_____

_____

What will you do?

_____

_____

_____

_____

_____

_____

Imagine you are Ellen Brock.

How do you feel?

_____

_____

_____

_____

_____

What will you do?

_____

_____

_____

_____

_____

_____

Techno-Tips

Dos and Don'ts of E-Mail

Most people now make use of E-mail in both their personal and work lives, and many organizations have internal E-mail systems. The company or organization may provide an E-mail account or smaller groups may just have lists of people in the organization, lists that everyone in the group can access. Here are some facts to think about when you are using the company's E-mail.

Most of the time people have no problem using E-mail and knowing how to use it correctly. Sometimes, however, people do get into trouble. Here are some pointers to remember:

1. Read your E-mail regularly.

2. If notices about meetings or other general events are sent by E-mail, be sure to add them to your calendar of things to do.

3. Answer questions promptly. Be to the point in your answer.

4. No one can hear your tone of voice in an E-mail. If you think you are saying something that's funny, you had better be sure it doesn't depend on your voice or a facial expression. People may take you seriously when you thought you were joking.

5. Anything you send on E-mail ends up in front of the person you sent it to. They can read it over and over again. This is not like a face-to-face conversation or even a telephone conversation that usually disappears (unless recorded) as quickly as it appears.

6. Not only can the intended receiver of your E-mail read it over and over, it is easy for that person to send it on to others with your name showing as the writer.

7. E-mail is not easily erased. Even when you delete it from your files, it is likely to be retrievable from the hard drive of your computer.

8. If you are one of a group of people receiving an E-mail, if you click on the "reply all" button of your E-mail software, everyone who was on the list will get your answer. If you want only the writer to get the answer, click on the "reply only" button.

9. Using a company's E-mail to do other business or for illegal activities such as betting on sporting events or sending a threatening note will get you fired and possibly jailed.

Situation Study 7

Jane was very happy to get her new job at the county hospital. Her work was varied. Sometimes she helped out with a variety of clerical duties in the billing office. But she was also responsible for all the nonmedical supplies. That meant she had to keep track of the inventory, notice when supplies were getting low, and fill out the order slip for more. This responsibility was a part of her job she really liked.

There was only one tiny problem. Jane had two bosses. When she worked in the billing office, she reported to Jeff. Her supply duties were under the supervision of David. Most of the time, Jane did not think much about this situation. They both seemed to know what they wanted and she knew how to do both jobs. It was true that David was a bit more controlling, but Jane thought she could handle that. It's true she had missed some orders once or twice but things had always worked out okay. And Jeff was really cute. Jane liked working with him.

Then, earlier that day, just as Jane was turning over some work to Jeff, David came into the billing office. He began speaking to her without as much as an "Excuse me." "Jane," he spoke quietly but with annoyance in his voice and on his face, "we are completely out of the pads of Form 102. You know that Form 102 is essential for the assignment of temporary nurses. I've told you before, you'll have to do better than this! I'll have to get on the phone right away to the vendor. Maybe he can fill the order on an urgent basis. Please pay more attention." And with that David left.

Jane was fuming. David had hollered at her in front of Jeff. And he hadn't even given her a chance to explain. Of course, she knew she should have checked the supply of forms, but still . . .

Jane sat down at her desk. As she turned on the computer, she was still furious. She remembered that there was a list of all the clerical and administrative staff people in the hospital; everyone except doctors and nurses was on it. Jane opened up a new message and put the name of the list in the "To" column. Then she began to type:

Hello Everyone,
You may not know me because I only started here about a month ago. But I have had a really bad morning. My bosses are Jeff in billing and David in supplies. David really ticks me off. Just a few moments ago, he hollered at me in Jeff's office. I can't stand him. I hope he rots in H - - L!
Your new friend,
Jane

And she clicked on "Send."

Imagine you are David.

How do you feel?

_____

_____

_____

_____

_____

_____

What will you do?

_____

_____

_____

_____

_____

_____

_____

Imagine you are Jeff.

How do you feel?

_____

_____

_____

_____

_____

_____

_____

What will you do?

_____

_____

_____

_____

_____

_____

_____

Imagine you are the head of all administrative personnel in the hospital.
You are on the list and get the E-mail.

How do you feel?

_____

_____

_____

_____

_____

_____

_____

What will you do?

_____

_____

_____

_____

_____

_____

_____

Become a Part of the Organization

Becoming a part of the organization is the last skill for success discussed because it is the most difficult one to explain. Daniel Goleman, a psychologist who has written extensively on how people get along in all kinds of organizations, says that people have to learn "what to say, what not to say, and what to call it."

If you think about your family for a few minutes, you may be able to understand what he means. Are there words you are not allowed to use in front of your parents or grandparents even though everyone knows those words? Are there things that have happened to family members that no one speaks about?

The same is true in the "family," or culture, of each organization. There are certain things that are done, other things that are not done, things that are said, and other things that are not said. As you become more experienced in work, you will find it easier to figure these out in each new organization you work for.

In the second skill for success related to getting along with your boss, the idea of adaptability was mentioned. You thought about needing to learn if your boss likes to structure everything you do or if he or she wants you to do more things on your own. That adaptability is an aspect of becoming part of the organization.

Michael Faber was hired for the data processing division of a large organization. He was a beginning worker with a lot of varied tasks. One day, Dawn Hays, his boss, asked him to look over a program that wasn't working to see if he could find the problem.

After a few hours of work, Michael called his boss over and said, "I found the problem. You made a mistake here."

Dawn bristled. "What do you mean *I* made a mistake?"

Michael pointed to the line of the program that had been written incorrectly and said, "Here it is."

"Oh," Dawn said, "fix it," and walked away angrily.

Michael had figured out what to say, but not what to call it. The answer to the question of what was wrong with the program was not *who* had made the error, particularly if that person was the boss, but *what* the error was. Michael should have said something like, "The problem is in line 46. A comma was needed instead of a space."

Knowing what to talk about at work and how to talk about it is a skill everyone learns. Of course, this can be carried too far. If you learn that the people or organization for which you are working are doing something that is illegal or unethical, then you are *not* supposed to keep quiet about it. Even if revealing the circumstances means that you will lose this particular job, in the long run you are definitely the winner.

Summary Worksheet

This chapter helped you understand ten skills for success drawn from research about what employers want.

The ten skills give a picture of the ideal employee. Your job is to identify the skills you already have and build upon them and to examine the skills where you are weaker so that you can strengthen your chances for success. Remember as you approach this, however, that nobody is perfect.

Put a check next to each skill you think you already have and a question mark next to those you want to work on.

_____ I am dependable.

_____ I know how to work well with my supervisor.

_____ I know when to ask questions and when not to.

_____ I can work cooperatively with my coworkers.

_____ I carry out my responsibilities.

_____ I take pride in what I do.

_____ I have initiative. I like to learn new skills and take on new tasks.

_____ I look my best on the job.

_____ I can control my emotions on the job, and I have learned some ways of dealing with stress away from work.

_____ I understand what it means to become a part of the organization.

CAREER CHANGES | Part III

Moving Up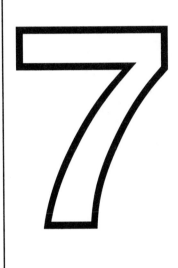

This part of the book is for the future. The first two parts concentrated on getting and keeping your first job. However, the chances are that you will not want things to stay the same forever. If all goes well, you will look for a raise, a promotion, or a new opportunity. Some times, in spite of our best efforts, life does not go as planned. Businesses close or particular positions are eliminated. Sometimes circumstance makes us change.

There are two chapters in this part of the book. This chapter is about opportunities within your current organization. It is about getting a raise on your first job and looking for a promotion within the same company. The next chapter takes you outside your current organization.

Getting a Raise

In the last chapter, you identified and learned how to apply ten skills for success. You are probably in line for a raise if you have worked on all these areas and your company or organization gives raises based on merit.

In some organizations, raises are based solely on length of employment. Each year you are there you get a specified salary raise, up to a certain point. This is true of many civil service jobs. In addition, for many civil service jobs the first period of employment (anywhere from six months to three years, depending on the job) is considered a probationary period. In the probationary period, you can be let go without the same kind of hearing and rights that you would have once you become a permanent employee. Your goal, if you want to remain on the job, is to become a permanent employee. If the job you hold is included in a collective bargaining agreement, then the salary increments each year are determined through negotiations between the union and your employer.

In some cases, there is a combination of a union scale and merit pay. Everyone gets at least the basic salary for the job and the number of years employed, but there is an opportunity to add merit pay. In general, it is the supervisor who puts in the request for merit pay for an employee.

If you are in an organization that does not have a standard salary schedule, there may still be a set period of review. Usually this review comes once a year. During the review period, you will discuss your accomplishments of the past year and your goals for work for the coming year. This is the point at which you can ask for a raise.

In some companies, there is no set pattern for salaries. Each person is on his or her own. It is appropriate to wait about a year after you are hired before asking for a raise. When you ask for a raise, the request should be based on your work and accomplishments. Do not talk about your financial need or obligations. You might also do some homework ahead of time to try and find out what raises people who are in jobs similar to yours have gotten. This will give you a clue as to what to expect, or if you are asked, to tell what you want.

Before you ask for a raise, you need to think about your accomplishments in the past year. To help you do that, complete the Raise Request Worksheet that follows. When you go in for that raise, be sure you remember your answers to the worksheet questions. Use them in your request.

Raise Request Worksheet

1. What new responsibilities have you taken on since you were hired?

_____

_____

_____

_____

2. What new skills have you acquired that you are now using on the job?

_____

_____

_____

_____

3. What special projects or activities were you involved in?

_____

_____

_____

_____

4. How did your work contribute to the product or service of the organization?

_____

_____

_____

_____

5. What praise or positive feedback have you received from your supervisor or others in the organization?

_____

_____

_____

_____

Getting Promoted

Perhaps you want more than a raise. A year or two have passed, and you have been getting signals from your supervisor and others within the organization that there may be an opening higher up for you.

To be sure that you are ready to take advantage of any opening, you need to know your organization. Some companies have *career ladders*. A career ladder is a path that many people are expected to take. There are, however, fewer and fewer positions as the rungs get higher. An example of a career ladder could be moving from typist in the pool, to secretary for a middle management executive, to office manager. Another career ladder is from sales clerk, to department manager, to a position in the management of the company as a whole.

If you are working for a large company, the personnel department or human resources department may have someone similar to a career counselor who is there to help you make your next moves within the organization. Keep in mind that, unlike a career counselor in school, this person is not very interested in helping you move *outside* the organization. You can ask if your organization has such a person or department, or you can watch for evidence of it. Usually if there is an active personnel department, you will see notices of jobs on bulletin boards or in company newsletters.

In addition to providing information on career opportunities, many companies will help you pay for additional education. Usually the courses you take or the degree you seek must be related to what you are doing and to the work of the company. If you have not completed college, you may be able to do so with a major in accounting or marketing or some other area of study useful to the company. If you have completed college, you may be able to take graduate level courses.

In some companies, the reimbursement is related to your grade in the course. An A will get you 100 percent reimbursement; a B, 75 percent; and so on. Again, you need to be observant and seek the information you want. You may have gotten a benefits booklet from the company and/or from a union when you were hired. Go back to that information now that you are ready for it.

In smaller organizations, the next step may not be clearly laid out for you. The best thing to do is to talk with your supervisor about what you might expect to do and how to prepare for it. By keeping your eyes open, you may see opportunities.

If you want to move up in your company, you will need to find out the procedures that are followed. These may include completing applications or presenting resumes. There may be interviews just as for your first job. Look over the information in Chapters 3 and 4 on "papers" and "people" to refresh your memory about these matters. Also look ahead at the next section of this chapter, which gives you some advice on applications, resumes, and interviews to use after you have had the experience of your first full-time, paid job.

In the Promotions Opportunity Worksheet that follows, there are some questions you can use to assess the opportunities for you in the company where you are now working.

Techno-Tip

Company Job Openings

Use your company's website or intranet to identify new opportunities in your field.

Promotions Opportunity Worksheet

1. Is there a human resources management department within my organization?

_____

2. Does it provide any help on promotions?

_____

3. Is there a bulletin board where I work that shows opportunities for promotion?

_____

4. Is there a company or union newsletter that shows opportunities for promotion?

_____

5. Is there a company website that posts promotion opportunities?

_____

6. Here are some opportunities that interest me:

a. _____

b. _____

c. _____

7. For which of those opportunities am I qualified?

_____

_____

_____

8. What can I do to improve my qualifications?

_____

_____

_____

9. What help can I get from the company with my education?

_____

_____

_____

10. What procedures do I follow to get the promotion I want?

_____

_____

_____

Summary Worksheet

This chapter helped you examine ways you can move ahead within your own organization. Use the checklist that follows to be sure you understand how to be successful in asking for a raise or seeking a promotion.

_____ I know my company policy on raises.

_____ I know why I deserve a raise.

_____ I can document the contributions that have earned me the right to ask for a raise.

_____ I have examined the right time to ask for a raise.

_____ I have planned how and when I will ask for a raise.

_____ I know how to show that I am qualified for a promotion.

_____ I have looked at the opportunities for promotion within my organization.

_____ I know which jobs I am qualified for by my experience and education.

Moving On

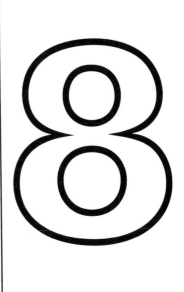

This chapter is about a bigger break—leaving the organization in which you held your first full-time job. The first section of the chapter reviews job-seeking skills. It adds some tips on how you can use the experience you have gained in your new job search. You will see how to fill out applications, complete a resume, and answer interview questions. The last part of the book encourages you to find your own path.

Finding a New Job

If you have decided that there are no opportunities for the promotion you want within the organization where you are now working, it is time to move on. This means you have to take out and dust off the job-hunting skills and strategies that were discussed at the beginning of this book.

The second chapter of this book talked about how to locate jobs. There is nothing new to add to your skills, but you have added a lot of people to those you knew before. While you may not want to advertise to everyone in your present organization that you are thinking about leaving, there may be some people you have met on the job or through the job who can help you. Add those people to your network. Then use all the resources you have—school placement offices, employment agencies, state employment services, newspaper ads, and networking.

The knowledge needed to fill out a job application will not change; nor will the need to be accurate, definite, honest, and complete; to read directions; and to complete the application neatly. You still need to think through your education and work histories and all your dates and places again. However, the information for your job application will change because you will now have a full-time, paid position to enter in the work history area.

Before you go to complete your first job application, think about how you can fill in your duties and responsibilities. You will have very little space to say all that you have done in the last year or two. Practice getting your description down to the fewest possible words.

In addition, you now have to answer the question, "Reason for Leaving," with something other than "Returned to school." It is important that you do *not* give a negative answer like "Could not get along with my boss," "Disliked my fellow workers," or "My boss was stupid." Surely there is some positive reason you are leaving, such as "Seeking a better-paying position" or "Desire promotion with more responsibility."

Finally, you will probably have different references to give. Try to find references that are as business-related as possible. You usually cannot list your immediate supervisor because that person is already listed in your work history section. However, if you have had good relations with other supervisors in your organization or you have gotten to know clients or customers of the organization you have been with, you can list them. Be sure you consider whether the person you are listing knows you well enough to give you a good reference. Be sure to ask for permission in person, by telephone, or by mail or E-mail before you list anyone.

In Chapter 3, we saw the application of Sandra Yee, who had graduated from community college with an associate's degree in accounting and was looking for a job as a bookkeeper. Sandra got that job and continued in college to complete her bachelor's degree. Sandra's new application form is filled out on the pages that follow.

Sample Job Application Form

Date of Application _____7-1-04_____ Social Security No. _____123-45-6789_____

Full Name (Last, First) _____Yee, Sandra_____

Address _____6105 Dawn Road_____

City _____Indianapolis_____ State _____Indiana_____ Zip _____46240_____

Home Telephone _____(317) 555-1010_____ Business Telephone _____(317) 555-1000_____

Position Applied For _____Accountant_____

Referred By _____newspaper advertisement 6-30-04_____

When will you be available to begin work? _____two weeks after hiring_____

Can you travel if the job requires it? _____yes_____

Have you been employed here before? _____no_____ If yes, give date _____—_____

Have you applied for a job here before? _____no_____ If yes, give date _____—_____

Are you a United States citizen? _____yes_____

If no, do you have an alien registration card and will you produce it for inspection? _____—_____

If you are a veteran of the U.S. Military Service, give dates of service and branch. _____na_____

Have you been convicted of a crime in the last seven years? _____no_____

If yes, give Date _____na_____ Place _____na_____ Offense _____na_____

Education:	Name and Address of School	No. of Years Attended	Did You Graduate?	Major/Degree
High School	Ripple HS 855 E. 59 St. Indianapolis	4	yes	Academic
College	Indiana University 900 W. New York St. Indianapolis	3	yes	Accounting
Trade School or Other	Indianapolis Community College 7331 Station St.	2	yes	Accounting

Special Training

_____

Employment History (Start with your most recent position)

Name & Address of Employer or Organization	Dates Employed from Month/Year to Month/Year	Nature of Work	Reason for Leaving	Name of Supervisor	Salary
General Supplies 3000 E. 48 St. Indianapolis	7 / 02 present	Bookkeeper	Seeking advancement	Marvin Brown	$33,000
Corn & More Supermarket 420 W. New York St. Indianapolis	9 / 00 5 / 02	Bookkeeper	Took full-time job	Neal McKinlay	$9.00 per hour
na					
na					

References (Other than supervisors listed above)

Name	Full Address	Telephone	Relationship
Linda Carey	Corn & More Supermarket 420 W. New York St. Indianapolis	555-1000	Owner of store
Duane Smith	Department of Accounting Indiana University 900 W. New York St.	555-4118	Professor
Carol Richmond	Department of Mathematics Indiana University 900 W. New York St.	555-4125	Professor

Special Skills (foreign languages, licenses, association memberships)

Familiar with IBM PC and use of spreadsheets

If you have ever been known by any other name, please indicate.

na

Just as you may have needed a resume for your first job, you may need one now. Review the five steps to a winning resume explained in detail in Chapter 3. If you want more information, use the book *How to Write a Winning Resume* (4th Edition) (VGM Career Books).

Five steps to a winning resume—a brief review

1. Examine the relevant areas of your life in depth.

2. Translate the details into action words and the vocabulary of work.

3. Write a rough draft of the resume.

4. Arrange your resume on the page so that it is easy to read and attractive.

5. Proofread your resume.

Just as with the application, there is no change in the process. What changes is your content. You need to put more emphasis on your accomplishments in your full-time, paid job and less on school activities and other accomplishments.

In Chapter 3, we saw the resume of Philip Jamison, who was looking for a job as an assistant to a buyer after he graduated from high school. He got the job and is now ready to move on. His resume after two years of experience is on the following page. Compare his two resumes. Then begin work on your resume. Remember that you will also need a cover letter to accompany the resume whenever you mail it.

Sample Resume—with Two Years of Work

Philip Jamison
571 Vermont Street
Brooklyn, New York 11207
(718) 555-3450

EDUCATION

Albert Einstein High School, Diploma, June 2002
Major: Merchandising
Specialized Courses: Retailing, Fashion Communications, Data Processing, Junior Achievement
Economics, Art Electives in Display and Package Design
Extracurricular Activities: School boutique purchase and sales committees

WORK EXPERIENCE

2002–2004   ASSISTANT TO THE BUYER   Ajax Merchandising Consortium
                 CHILDREN'S WEAR   New York, New York

Assisted in all aspects of purchasing of children's wear. Accompanied buyer to showrooms and participated in decision making. Carried out follow-up of orders by telephone and letters. Kept records of orders from retailers on an IBM PC. Worked with computer consultant to establish record keeping system that would track orders filled, orders to be filled, and merchandise available from wholesalers.

2000–2002   STOCK CLERK   Blooms Department Store
                                               New York, New York

Stocked shelves, monitored supplies on the floor. Took inventory. Assisted in unpacking and packing. (Part-time work while in school.)

Summer 1999   MAINTENANCE WORKER   Parks Department
                                               New York, New York

Participated in all indoor and outdoor cleanup activities in various parts of Central Park.

SKILLS

Familiar with the IBM PC and several data processing and word processing software packages.
Type 60 WPM.

You also have to prepare for job interviews as you did before. Look over Chapter 4 on interviewing. You will need to prepare yourself now as you did then. You were successful in getting your first job. The second one is usually easier to get. Now you have that thing that all employers say they want: *experience!*

It is your job to translate that experience into terms that will sound appealing to your next employer. He or she wants to be sure you are bringing something valuable that you gained on your last job and that you are not leaving because you failed. Employers like to see experience because they can use how you performed on your previous job to predict how you will do on your next job. Of course, unless you are going to work for someone who saw you at work, most of what they know will come from you.

Be prepared to answer questions about the job you have now—the one you are leaving. You can expect a question about why you want to change jobs. Avoid being overly critical of your previous boss or company. It makes the new employer worry that you will also be overly critical of her or him. Focus on your positive reasons for leaving. Do you want a job with more room for growth? Do you want a job with more responsibility and the higher rewards that go with it? Do you want to use the experiences you have had to meet new challenges?

Some other questions you may be asked that relate to your work are listed on the worksheet that follows:

Interview Questions About Your Job

1. What were your major experiences on your last job?

_____

_____

2. What did you learn on your last job that you can use here?

_____

_____

3. What was the biggest problem you faced on your last job?

_____

_____

4. How did you solve that problem?

_____

_____

5. What did you like best about your last job?

_____

_____

6. What did you like least about it?

_____

_____

7. What was your most rewarding experience at work?

_____

_____

Use the same principles and worksheets that you used to prepare for your first set of job interviews. You will find them in Chapter 4. There are more of them in the book *How to Have a Winning Job Interview* (3rd Edition) (VGM Career Books).

In addition, use the worksheet that follows to match your experience in your first job with the skills needed in the new job you are seeking.

Job-to-Job Worksheet

Current Job Responsibilities	Skill Acquired	New Job Responsibilities
Example : Prepared showroom display	Arrangement of products	Window arrangements
_____	_____	_____
_____	_____	_____
_____	_____	_____
_____	_____	_____
_____	_____	_____
_____	_____	_____
_____	_____	_____
_____	_____	_____
_____	_____	_____
_____	_____	_____
_____	_____	_____
_____	_____	_____
_____	_____	_____
_____	_____	_____
_____	_____	_____
_____	_____	_____
_____	_____	_____
_____	_____	_____
_____	_____	_____
_____	_____	_____
_____	_____	_____
_____	_____	_____
_____	_____	_____
_____	_____	_____
_____	_____	_____
_____	_____	_____

On Your Own   This book has presented a number of ways of getting-and keeping—your first job. However, no matter how many different examples we give, life itself can be more complicated. For example, in the chapter on career ladders, there was no discussion of the kind of person who jumps ahead quickly, skipping many steps and going from the mailroom to the president's office in a couple of quick leaps. Yet these things happen.

The best way to use this book is to decide what you want to do at any current stage in your life and then use the parts that apply. Not everyone wants to follow the same path. A good book about making your own path is *SoulWork: Finding the Work You Love, Loving the Work You Have* (Davies-Black).

You may want to work for a while and then stop and go to school, or you may want to work for someone else and then try a business of your own. You may see some way the organization you are working for can really do better and decide to sell that idea, breaking all the rules of who speaks to whom. Remember, you can do whatever you decide to do.

Perhaps instead of looking for promotions or raises, you would like to think about working for yourself, running your own business. There are many books about running each different kind of business. And there are websites as well. Get all the information you can before you make this decision.

A few last words—do not be in too much of a hurry by *always* thinking about how to get ahead. If every step in life is just to prepare you for the next step, when do you get to enjoy the step you are on?

Summary Worksheet

Look back over this chapter to be sure you know how to make the most of your experience when you begin to think about getting a new job. Use the checklist to be sure you have left nothing out.

———— I know how to go about finding a new job.

———— I have reviewed the information about job applications, and I have prepared a new worksheet with current information.

———— I have identified new references.

———— I have gone over the methods for writing a resume, and I have written a new one.

———— I have prepared a new cover letter.

———— I have prepared myself for an interview. I am ready to talk about how my experiences on my present job prepare me for my new job.

———— I have thought about my personal career direction and realize there are many alternatives open to me.

———— I am enjoying my career.

Resources

Books to Help You in Your Job Search

The Civil Service Administrative Handbook. ARCO, New York: 2000.

Creative Visualization. Shakti Gawain, Bantam Books, New York: 1979.

Here's How: Choose the Right Career. Louise Welsh Schrank, VGM Career Books, Chicago: 1991.

How to Have a Winning Job Interview, 3rd edition. Deborah P. Bloch, VGM Career Books, Chicago: 1999.

How to Make the Right Career Moves. Deborah P. Bloch, VGM Career Books, Chicago: 1990.

How to Write a Winning Resume, 4th edition. Deborah P. Bloch, VGM Career Books, Chicago: 1999.

Occupational Outlook Handbook. U. S. Department of Labor, VGM Career Books, Chicago: 2002–2003 edition.

The 7 Habits of Highly Effective People. Stephen R. Covey, Simon and Schuster, New York: 1989.

SoulWork: Finding the Work You Love, Loving the Work You Have. Deborah P. Bloch and Lee J. Richmond, Davies-Black, Palo Alto, California: 1998.

What Color Is Your Parachute? Richard Nelson Bolles, Ten Speed Press, Berkeley, California: 2001.

Useful Internet Sites

bls.gov/oco/home is the site of the Web-based *Occupational Outlook Handbook.* The OOH is compiled by the United States Bureau of Labor Statistics. It gives detailed information about the major occupations in the United States and provides links to related information about each of those occupations.

career-mosaic.com is a privately run Internet career resource center with many links within it.

careerpath.com lists the job ads from forty-five (at this writing) newspapers.

google.com, yahoo.com, and dogpile.com are general search engines that can be used to find websites of interest. Each one works on a different principle.

hotjobs.com lists jobs in technology in more than one hundred companies.

monster.com provides another database of jobs.

About the Author

Deborah P. Bloch, Ph.D., is the author of four books designed to help people find the jobs that are right for them. These books, all in the VGM Career Books series, have sold more than 150,000 copies. Dr. Bloch is also the author of books for individuals, counselors, and educators on the spiritual aspects of work, factors that enhance the sense of wholeness in career.

Dr. Bloch has focused her work on the career development of individuals and the organizational structures that promote a healthy work environment. She is Professor of Organization and Leadership at the University of San Francisco. Previously, she was at Baruch College of the City University of New York. In addition to her university work, Dr. Bloch has worked as a consultant in the United States and abroad. She has served as president of both the National Career Development Association and the Association of

Computer-Based Systems for Career Information. She is a member of the editorial board of the *Career Planning and Adult Development Journal.* Dr. Bloch has received the Distinguished Service Award of the Association of Computer-Based Systems for Career Information, the Resource Award of the Career Planning and Adult Development Network, and the Merit Award of the National Career Development Association.

Bloch's work includes many published professional articles and numerous workshops for counselors and others who help people with their career decisions and job searches.

Other books by Dr. Bloch include:

Published by VGM Career Books:

- *How to Write a Winning Resume* (now in its 4th Edition)

- *How to Have a Winning Job Interview* (now in its 3rd Edition)

- *How to Make the Right Career Moves* (suggestions for people in midcareer)

Published by Davies-Black Publishing:

- *SoulWork: Finding the Work You Love; Loving the Work You Have* (with Dr. Lee J. Richmond)

- *Connections Between Spirit and Work in Career Development: New Approaches and Practical Perspectives* (a set of original readings edited by Deborah P. Bloch and Lee J. Richmond)

Dr. Bloch would like to express her ongoing appreciation to Dr. Joyce H. Pinkney who most cheerfully and ably assisted in the preparation of the manuscript for this book.